Dogs!!

...of Kansas City!!

Photography
By Video Plus Photography

As of 2015, the American Kennel Club recognizes 184 breeds of dogs, although over 300 exist in the world. The pooches in this book (many of which are shelter dogs) were photographed at the Bark 4 Our Park 5K Doggie Dash in Liberty, Missouri, the Gladfest Dog Show in Gladstone, Missouri and at other locations in the North Kansas City area.

This book is dedicated to dogs and their owners throughout the world.

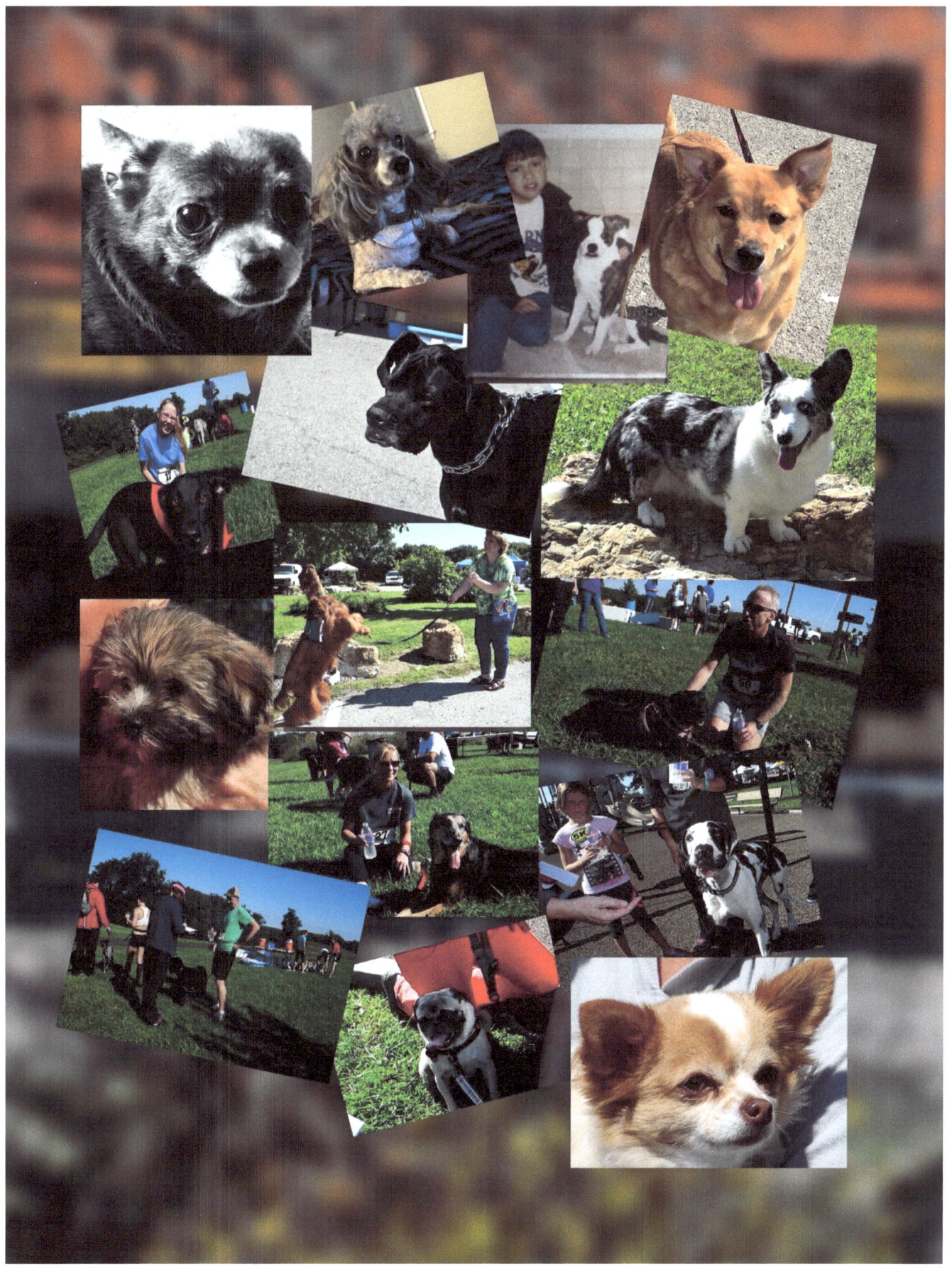

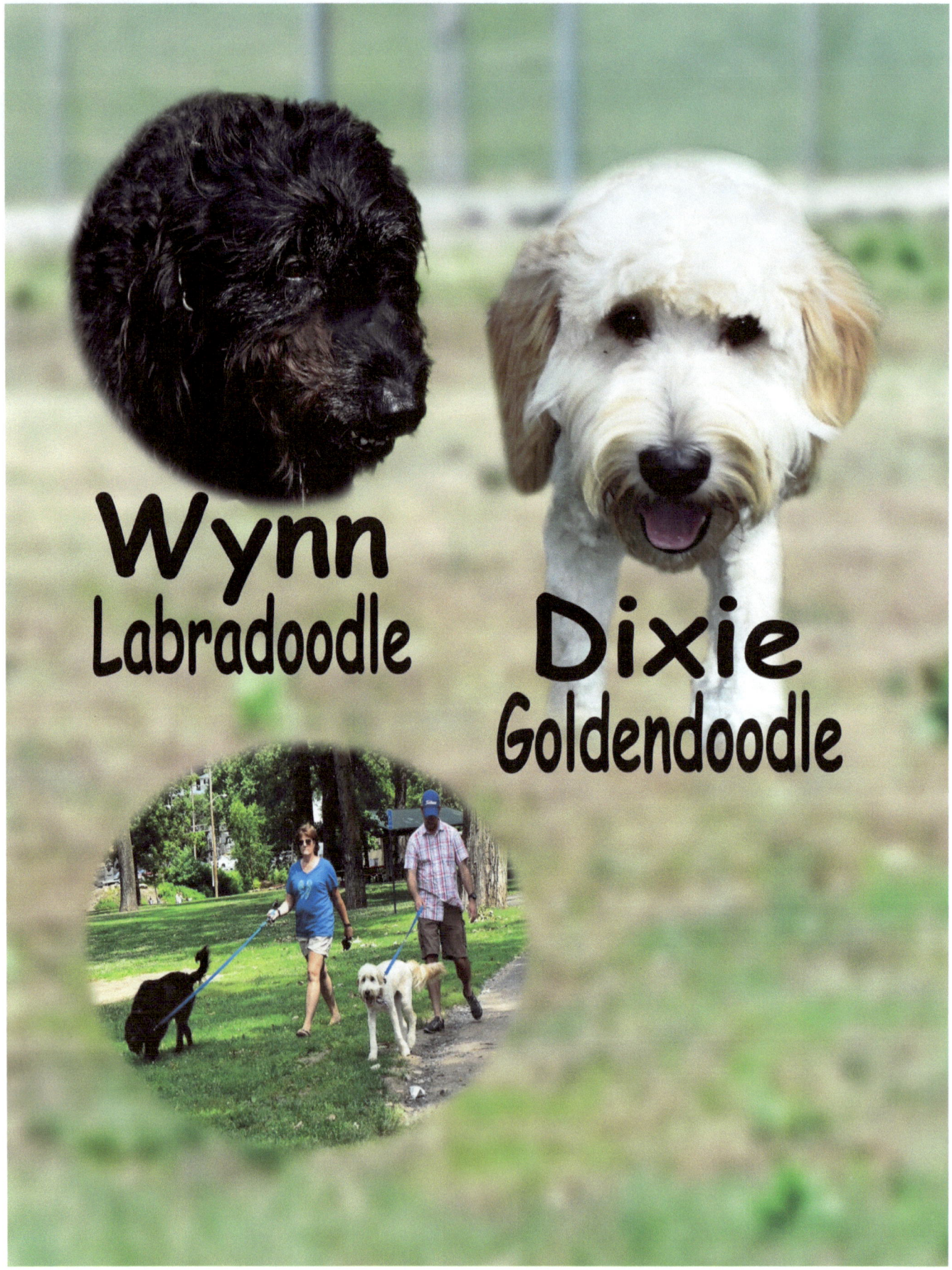

Wynn
Labradoodle

Dixie
Goldendoodle

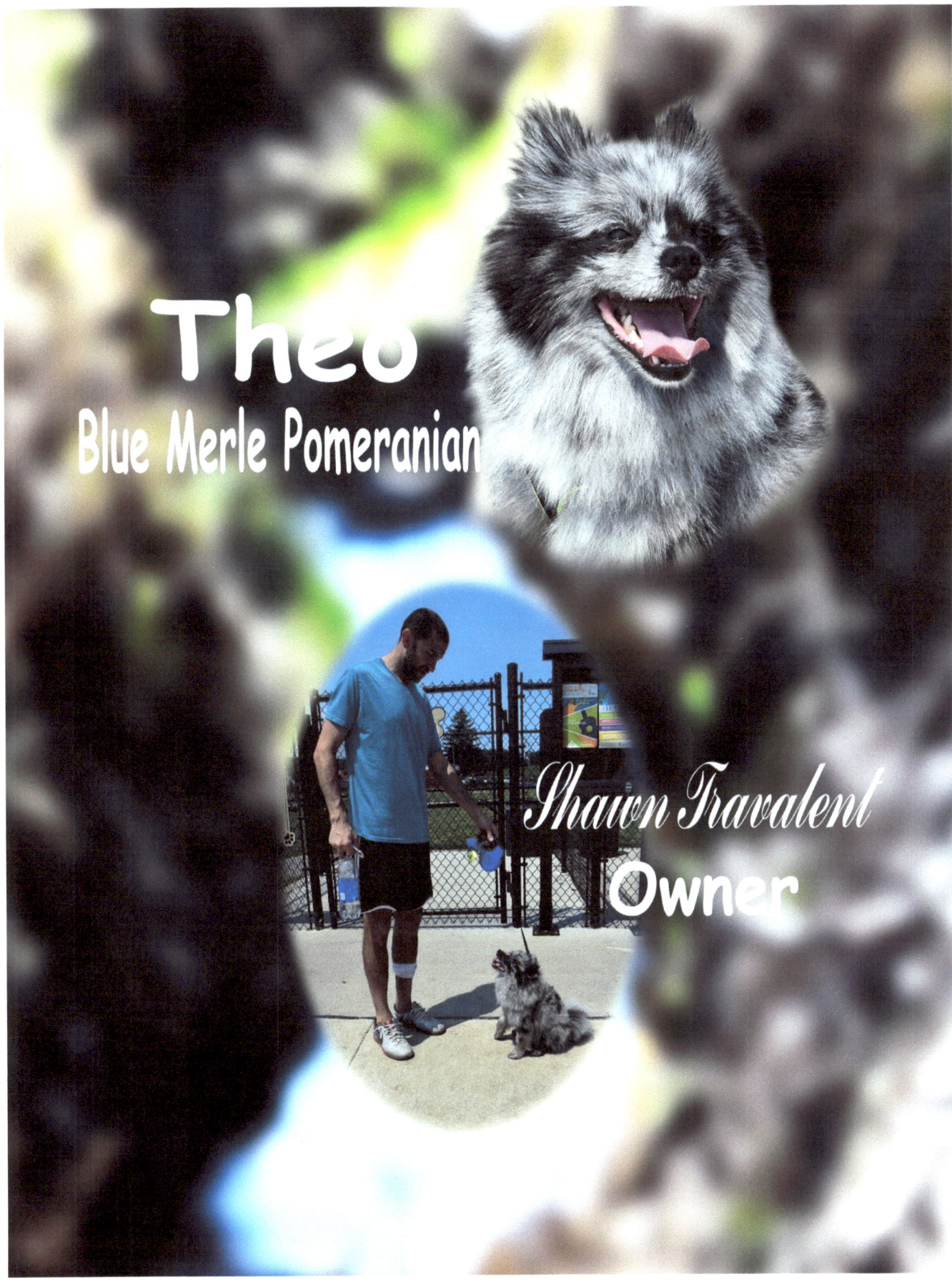

Theo
Blue Merle Pomeranian

Shawn Travalent
Owner

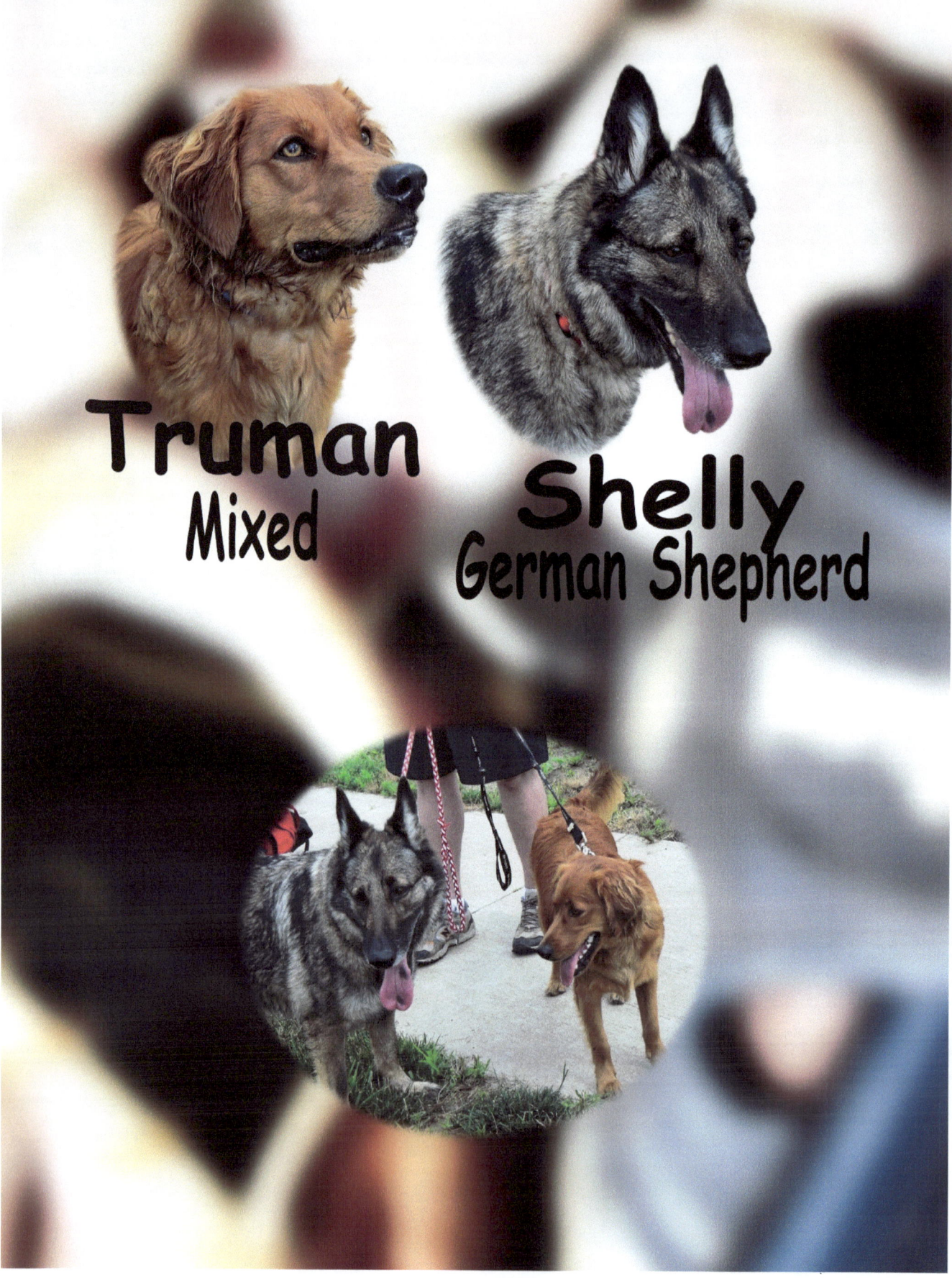

Truman
Mixed

Shelly
German Shepherd

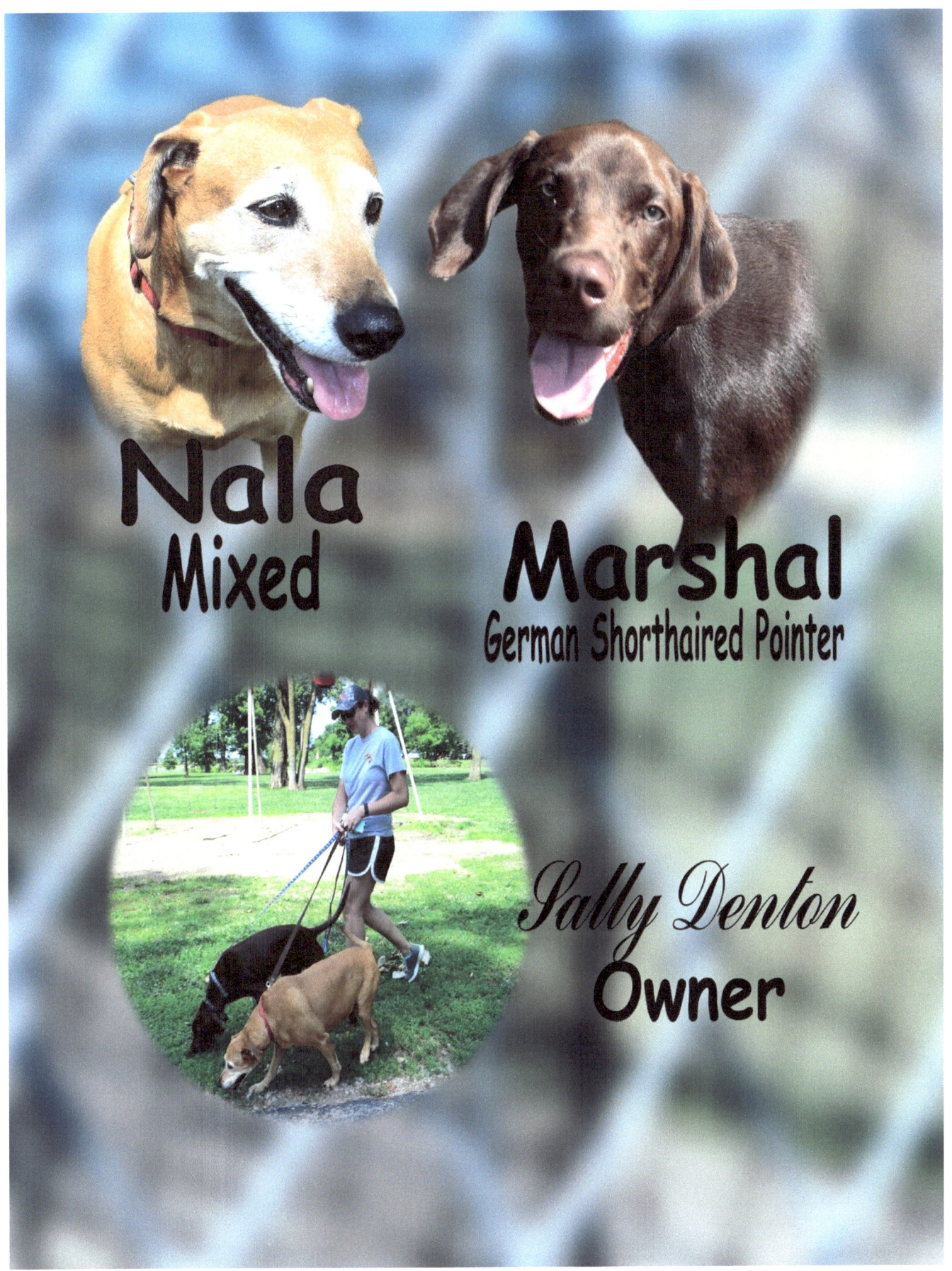

Nala
Mixed

Marshal
German Shorthaired Pointer

Sally Denton
Owner

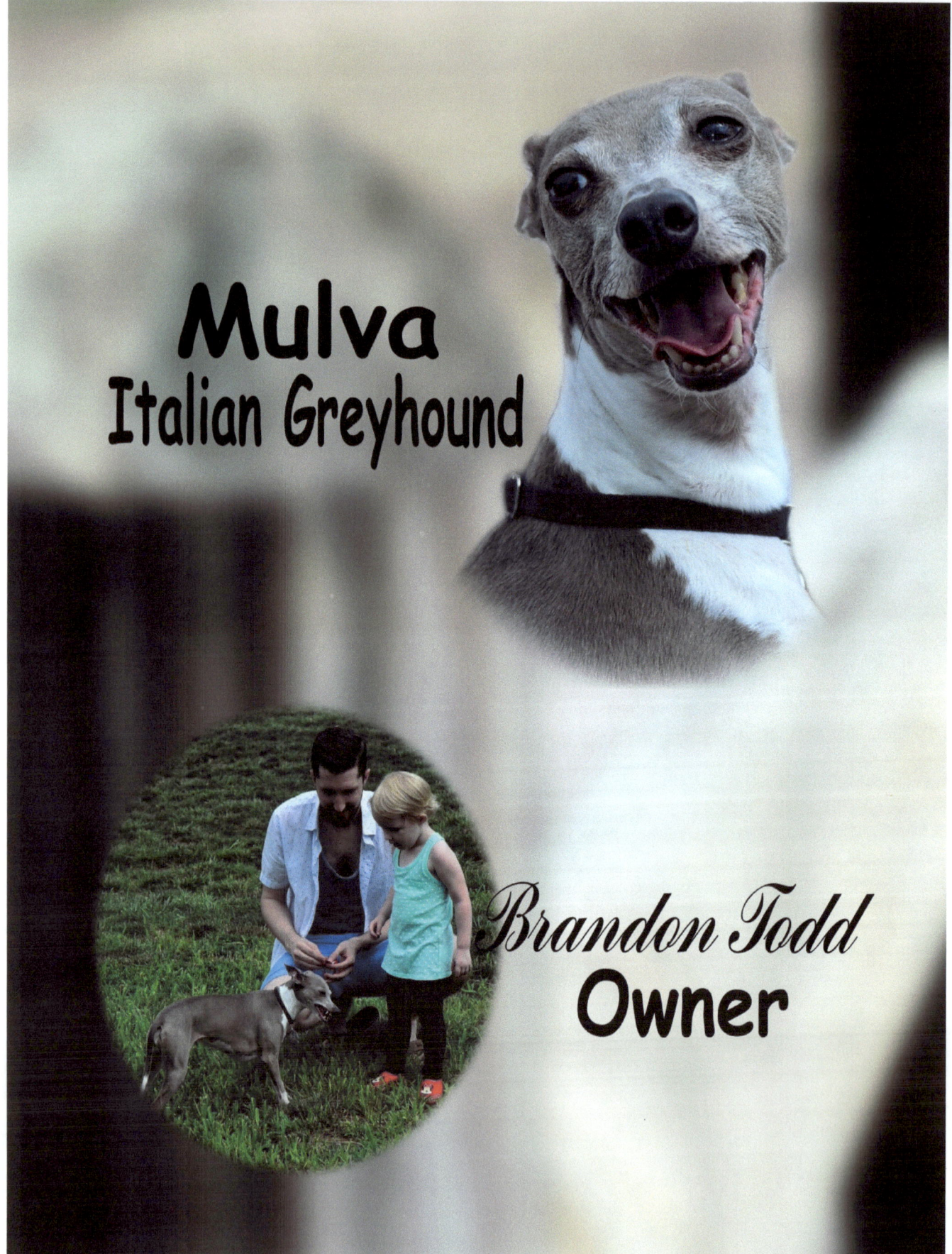

Mulva
Italian Greyhound

Brandon Todd
Owner

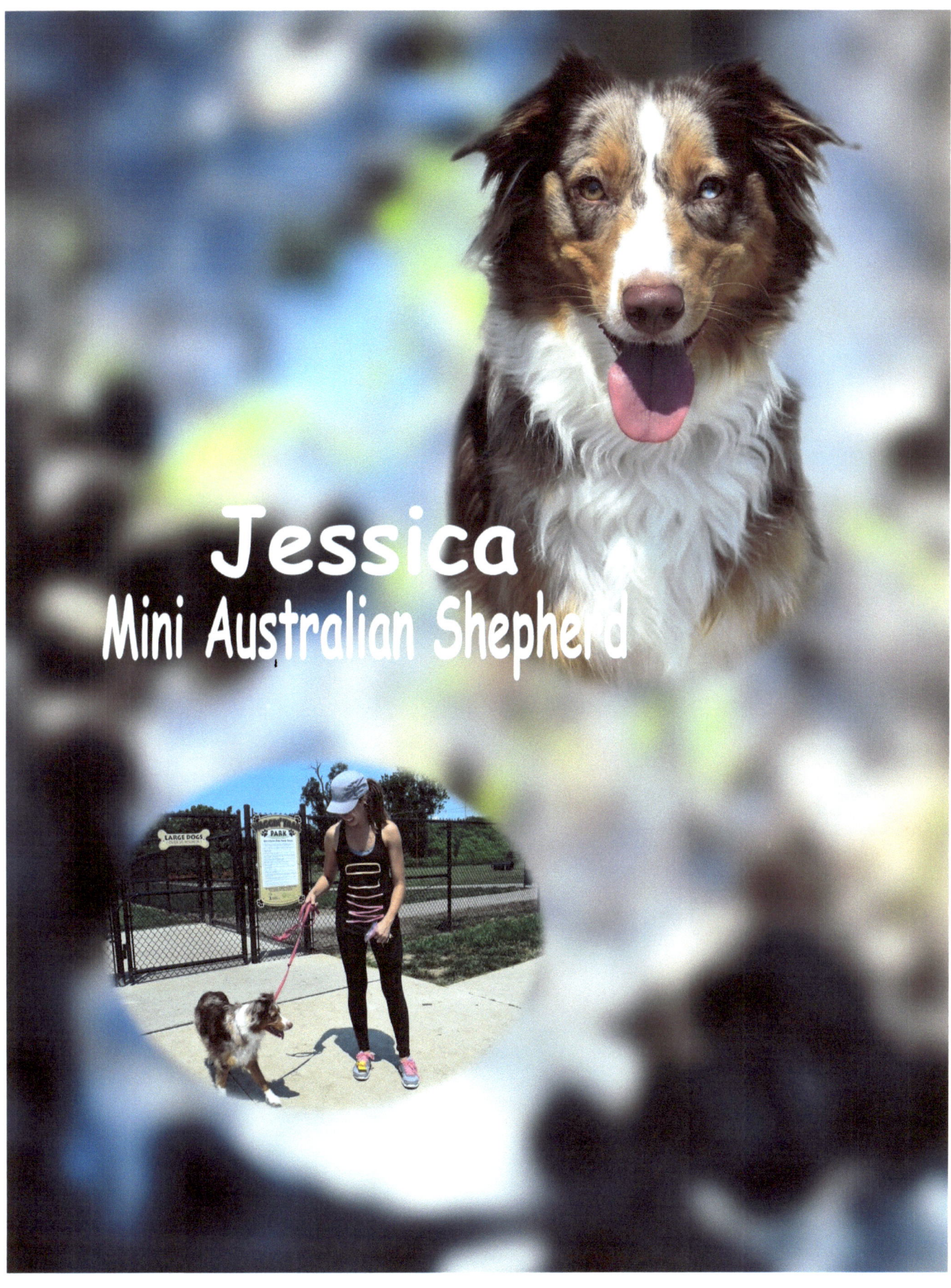

Jessica
Mini Australian Shepherd

Skydeck Publishing

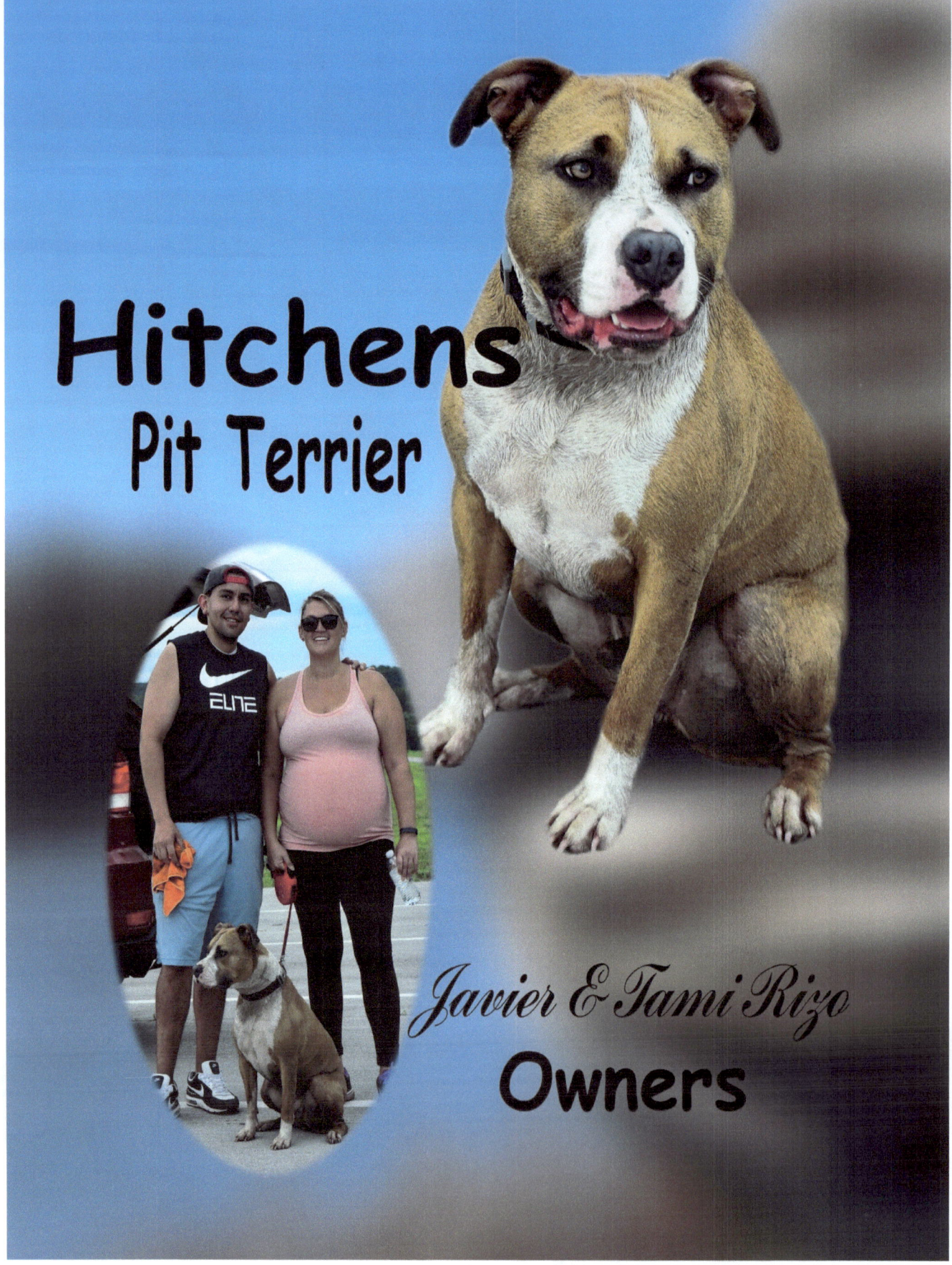

Hitchens
Pit Terrier

Javier & Tami Rizo
Owners

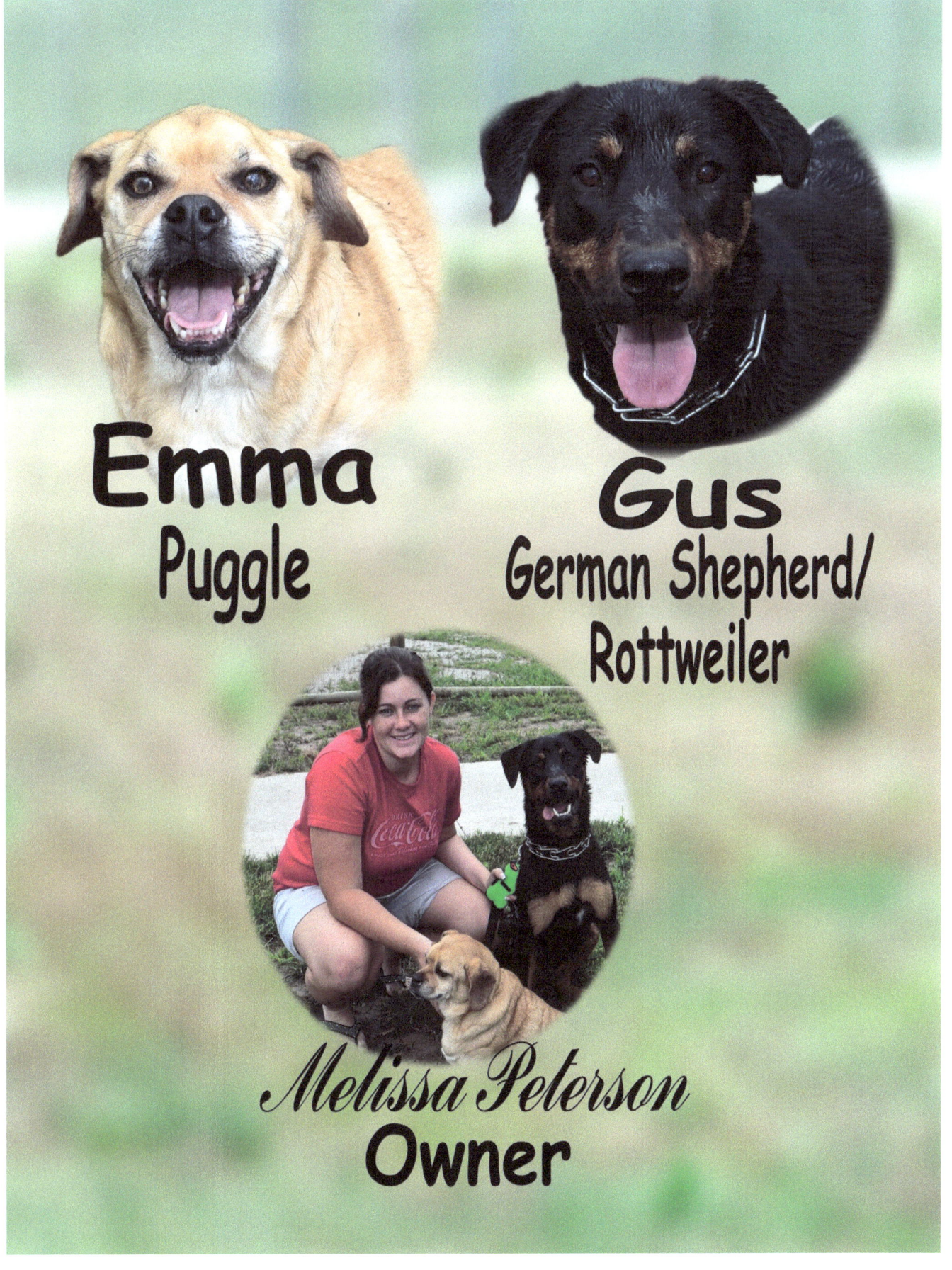

Emma
Puggle

Gus
German Shepherd/
Rottweiler

Melissa Peterson
Owner

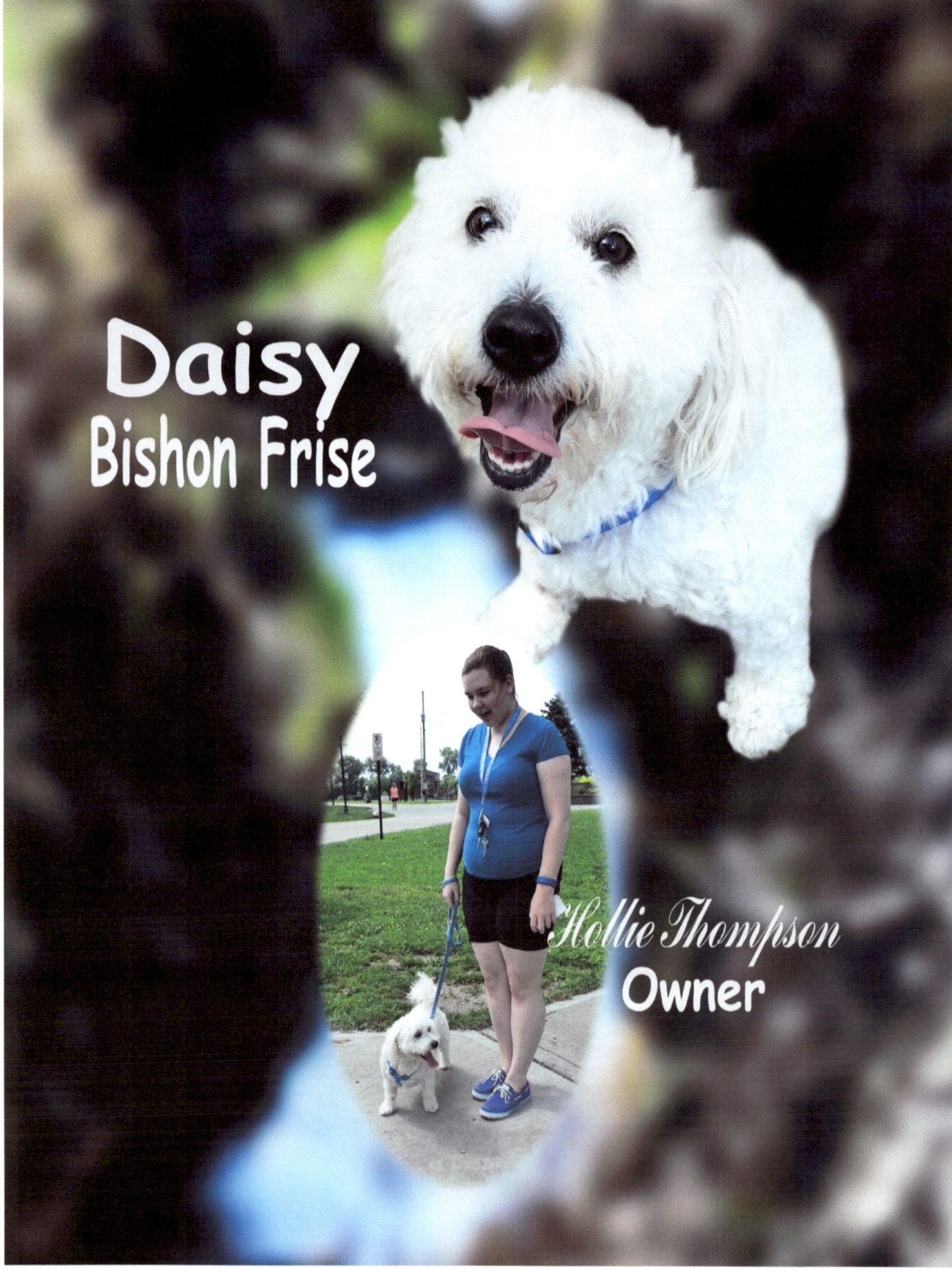

Daisy
Bishon Frise

Hollie Thompson
Owner

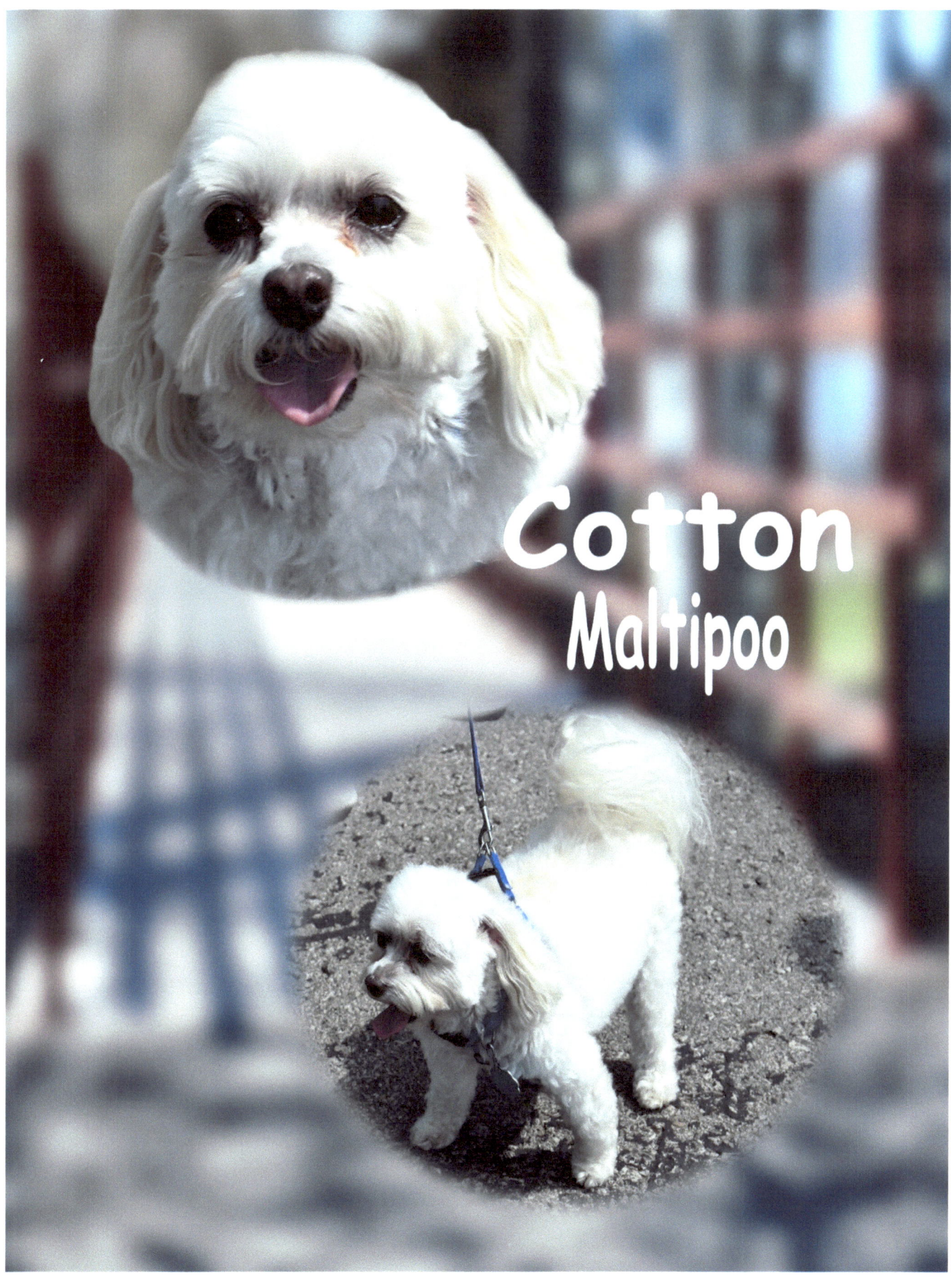

Cotton
Maltipoo

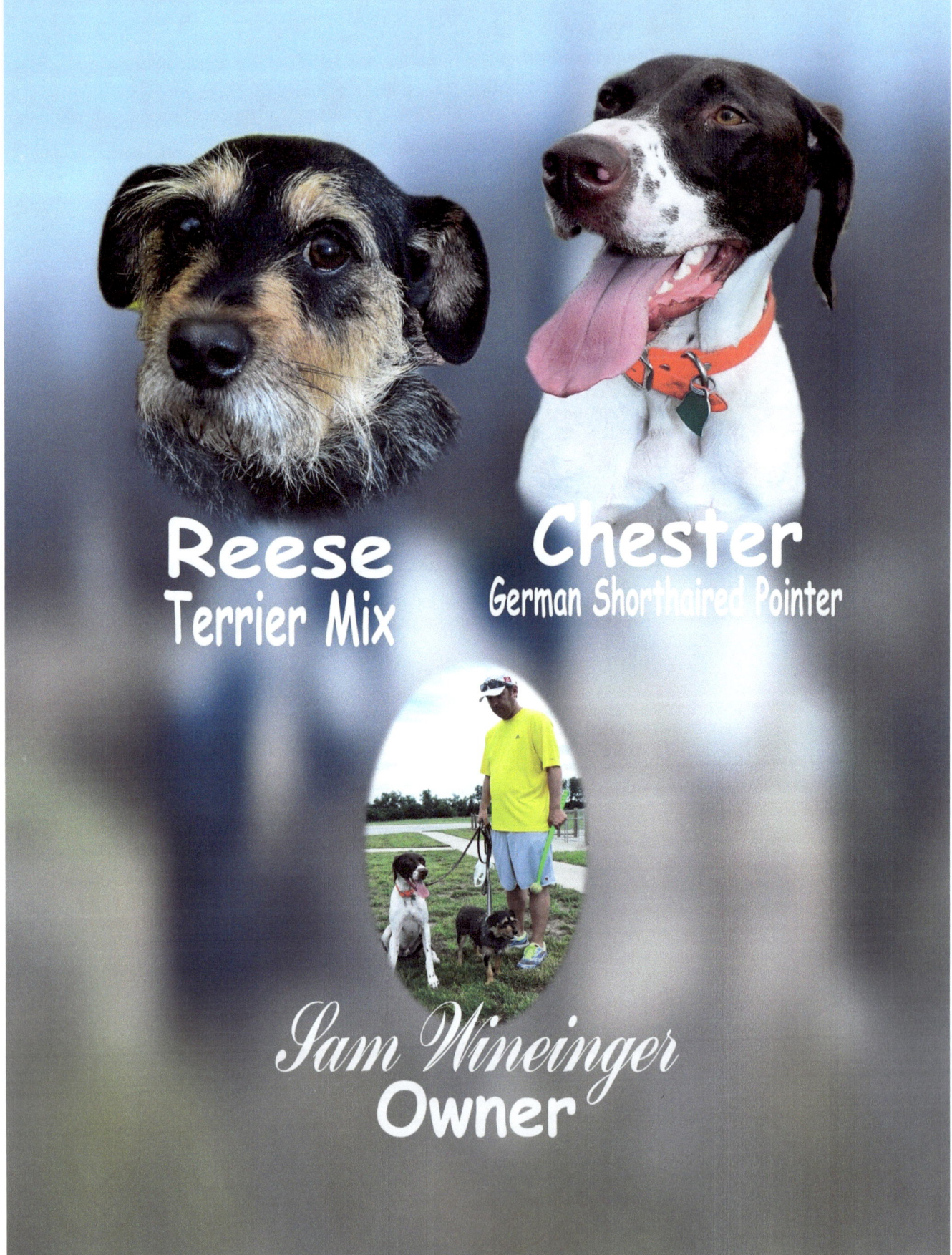

Reese
Terrier Mix

Chester
German Shorthaired Pointer

Sam Wineinger
Owner

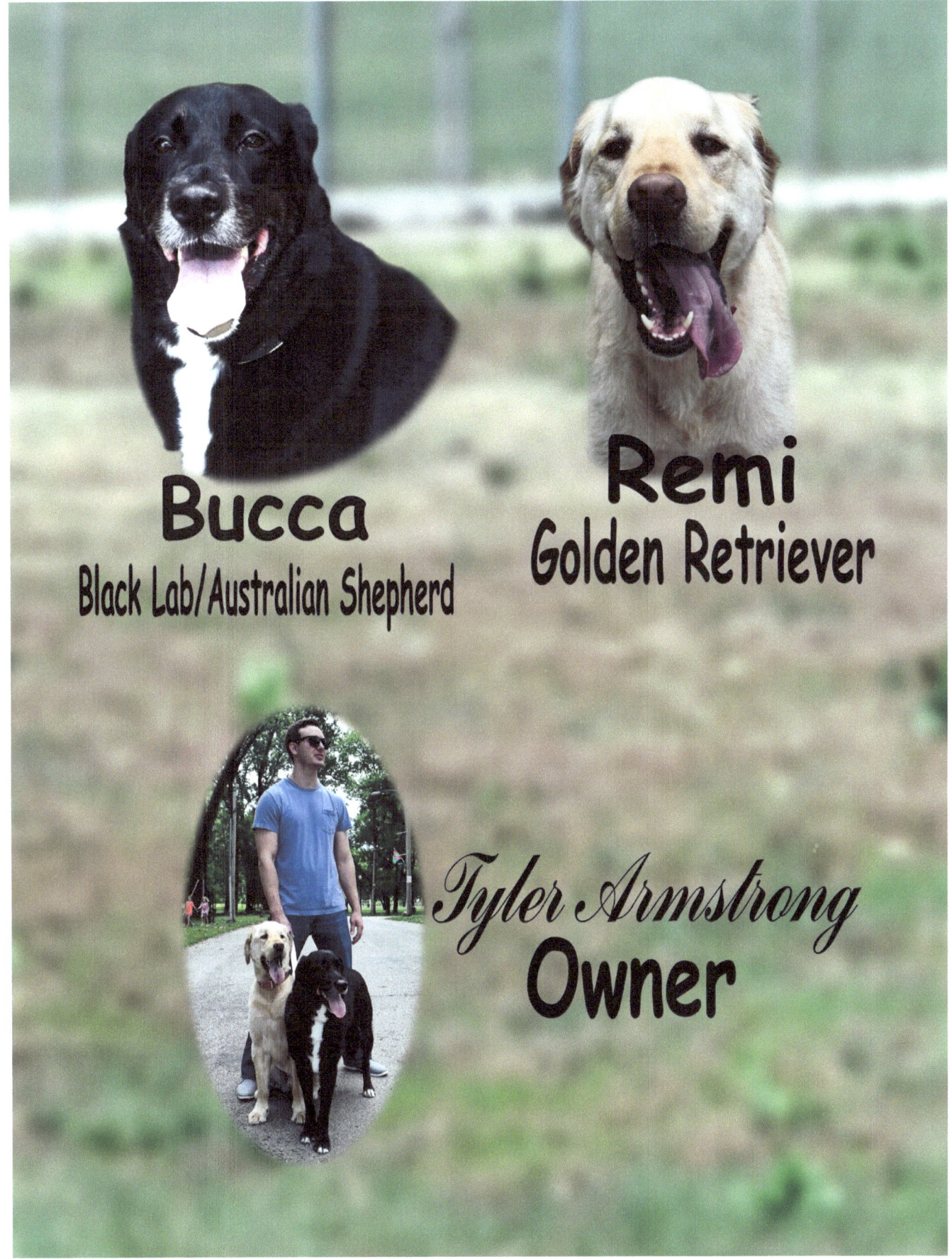

Bucca
Black Lab/Australian Shepherd

Remi
Golden Retriever

Tyler Armstrong
Owner

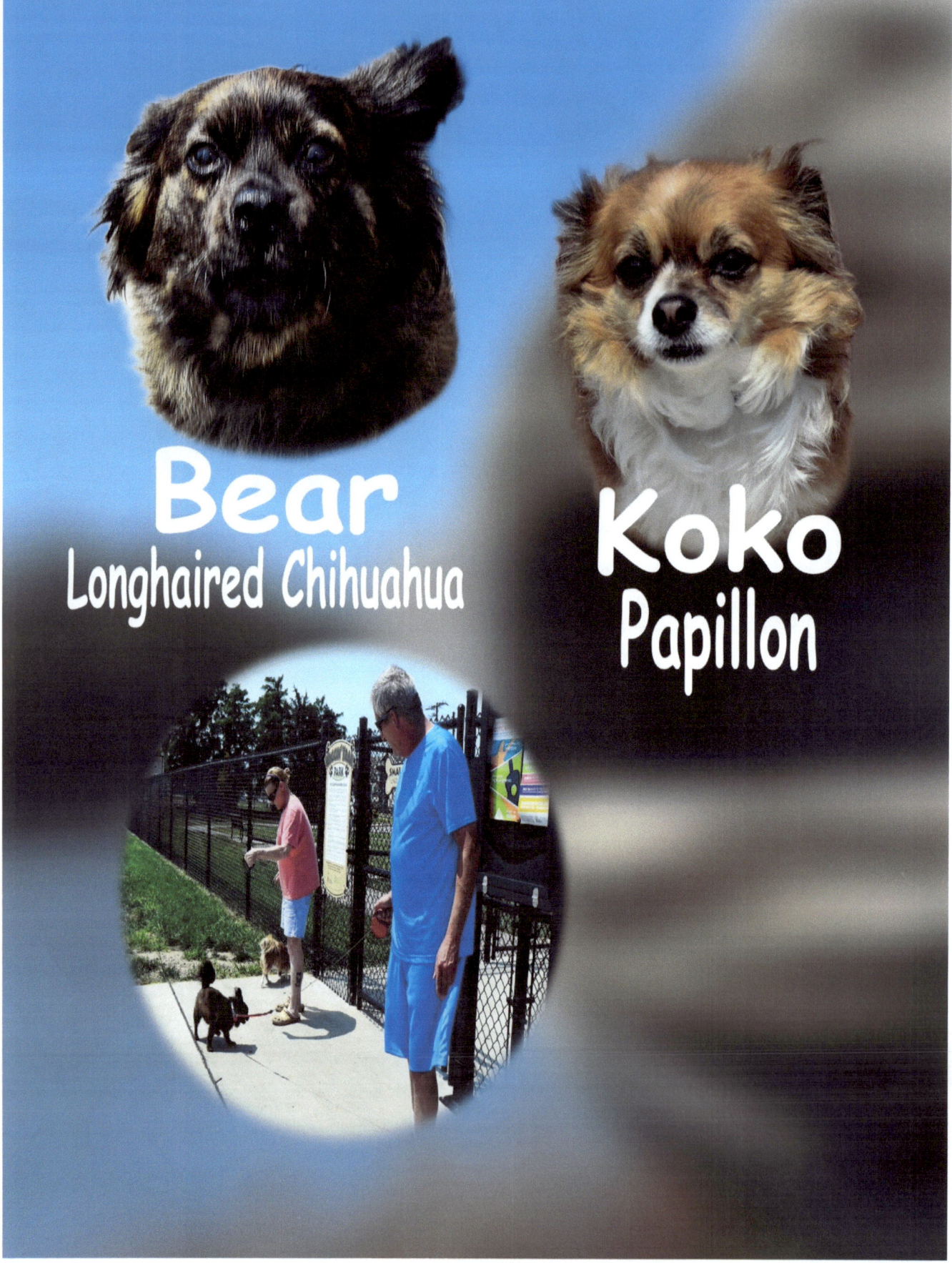

Bear
Longhaired Chihuahua

Koko
Papillon

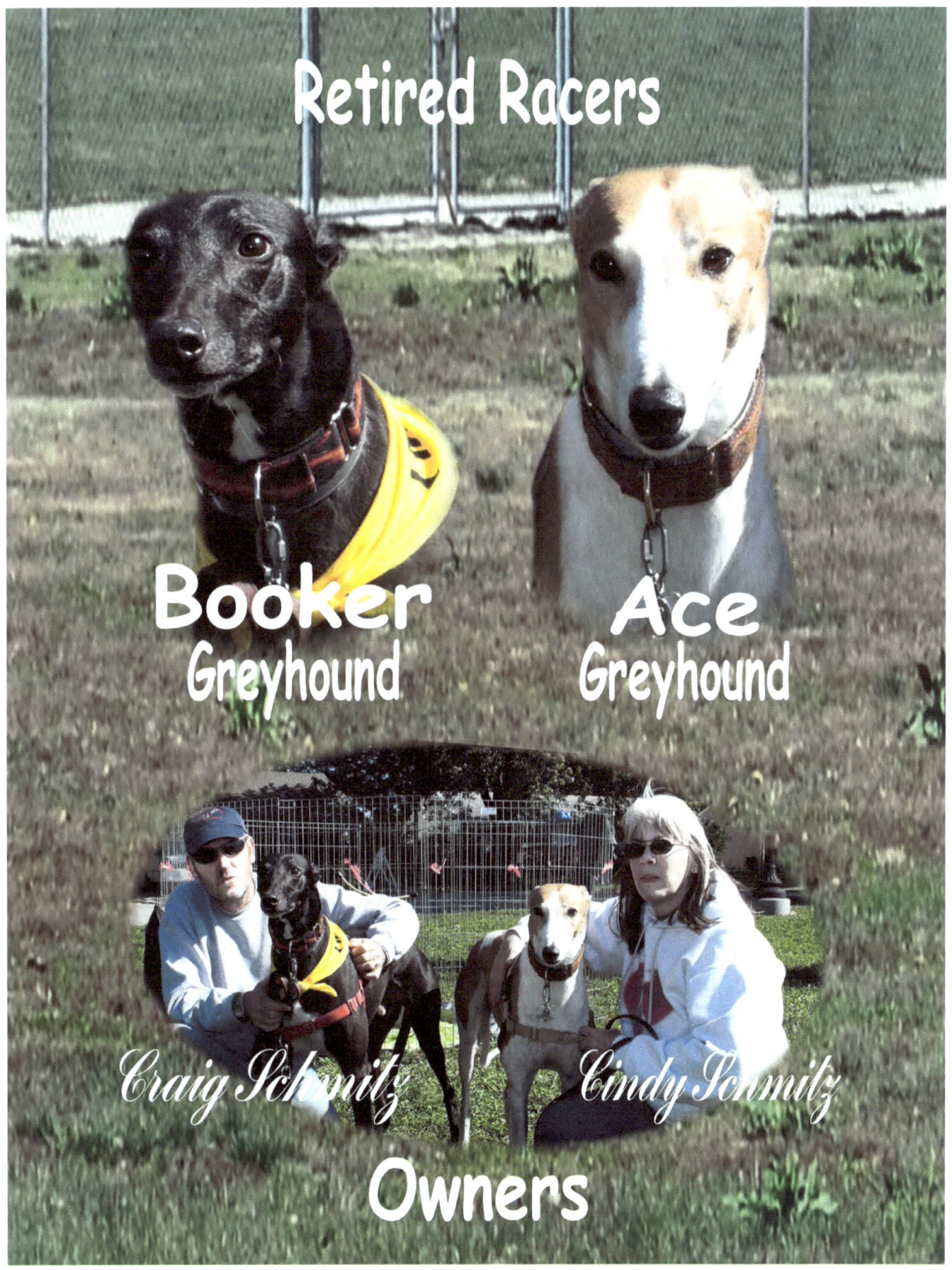

Retired Racers

Booker
Greyhound

Ace
Greyhound

Craig Schmitz

Cindy Schmitz

Owners

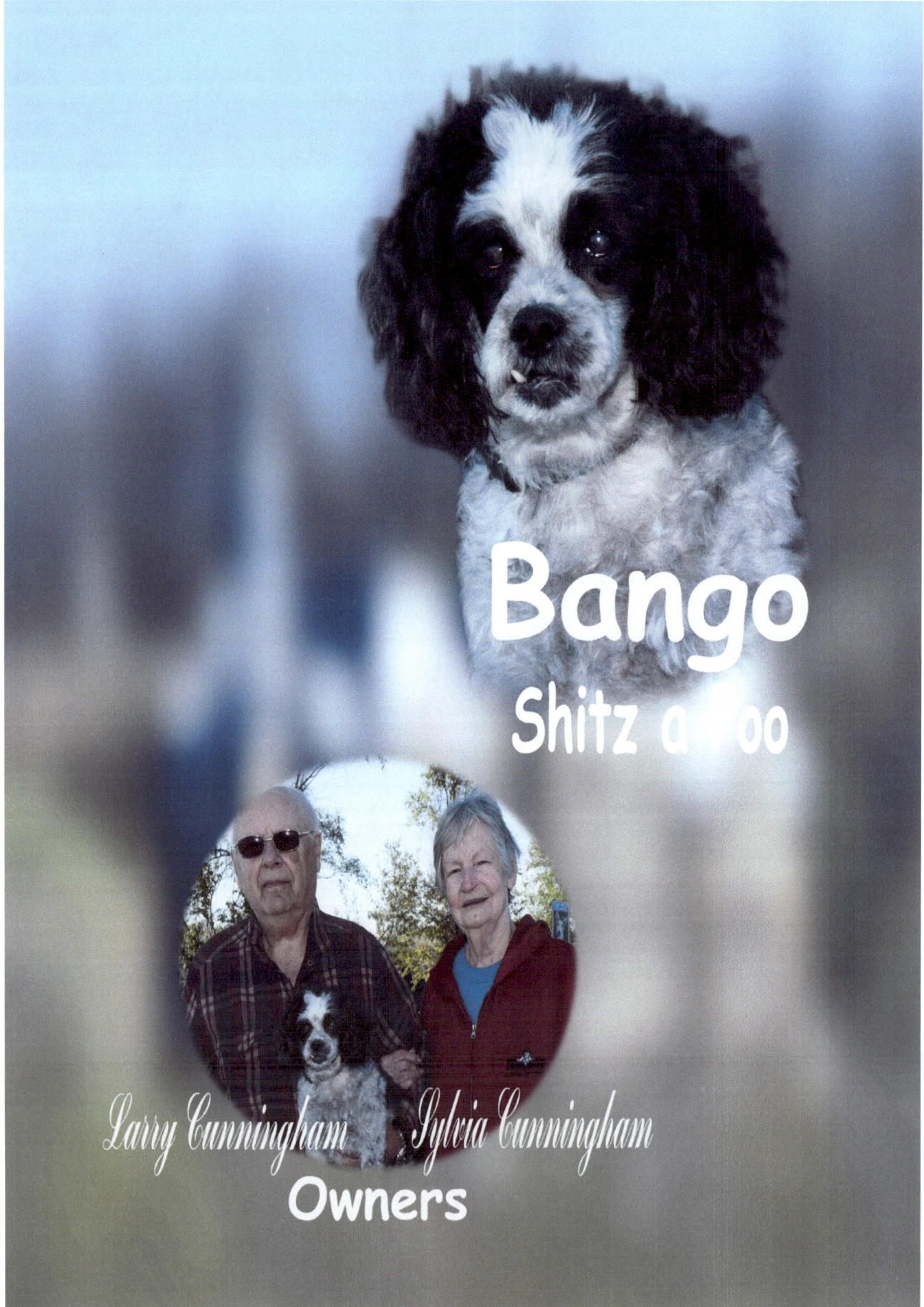

Bango
Shitz a Poo

Larry Cunningham   Sylvia Cunningham
Owners

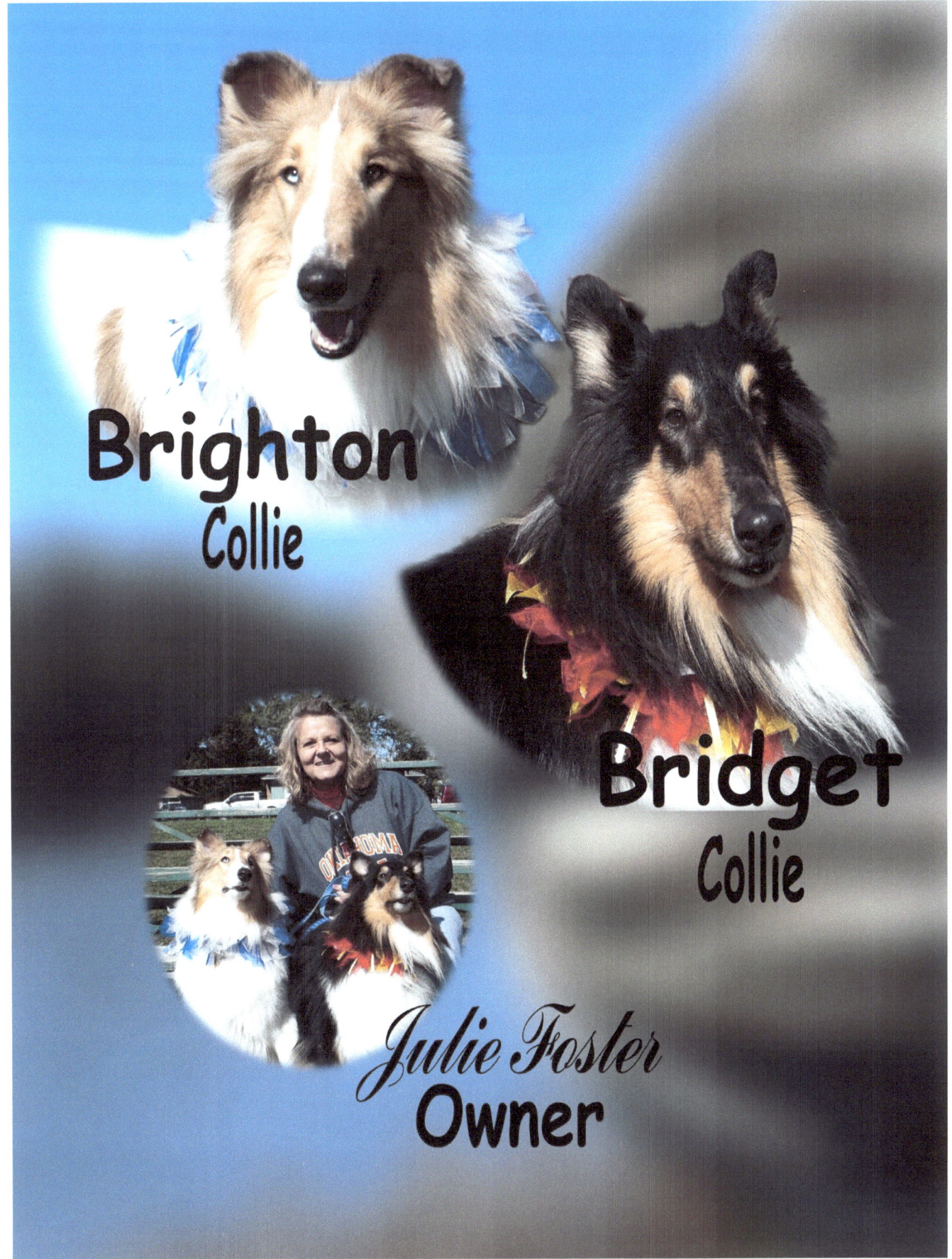

Brighton
Collie

Bridget
Collie

Julie Foster
Owner

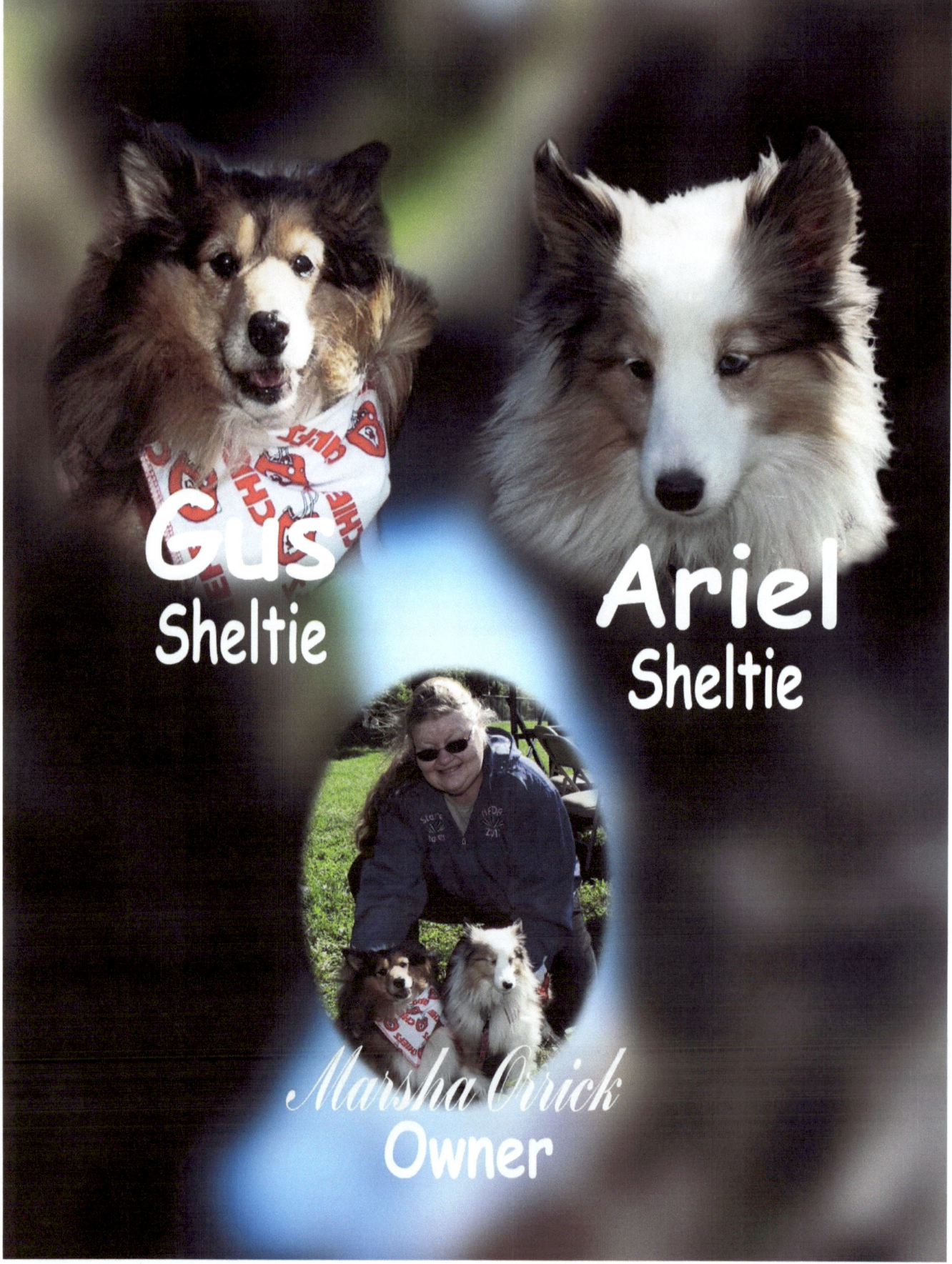

Gus
Sheltie

Ariel
Sheltie

Marsha Orrick
Owner

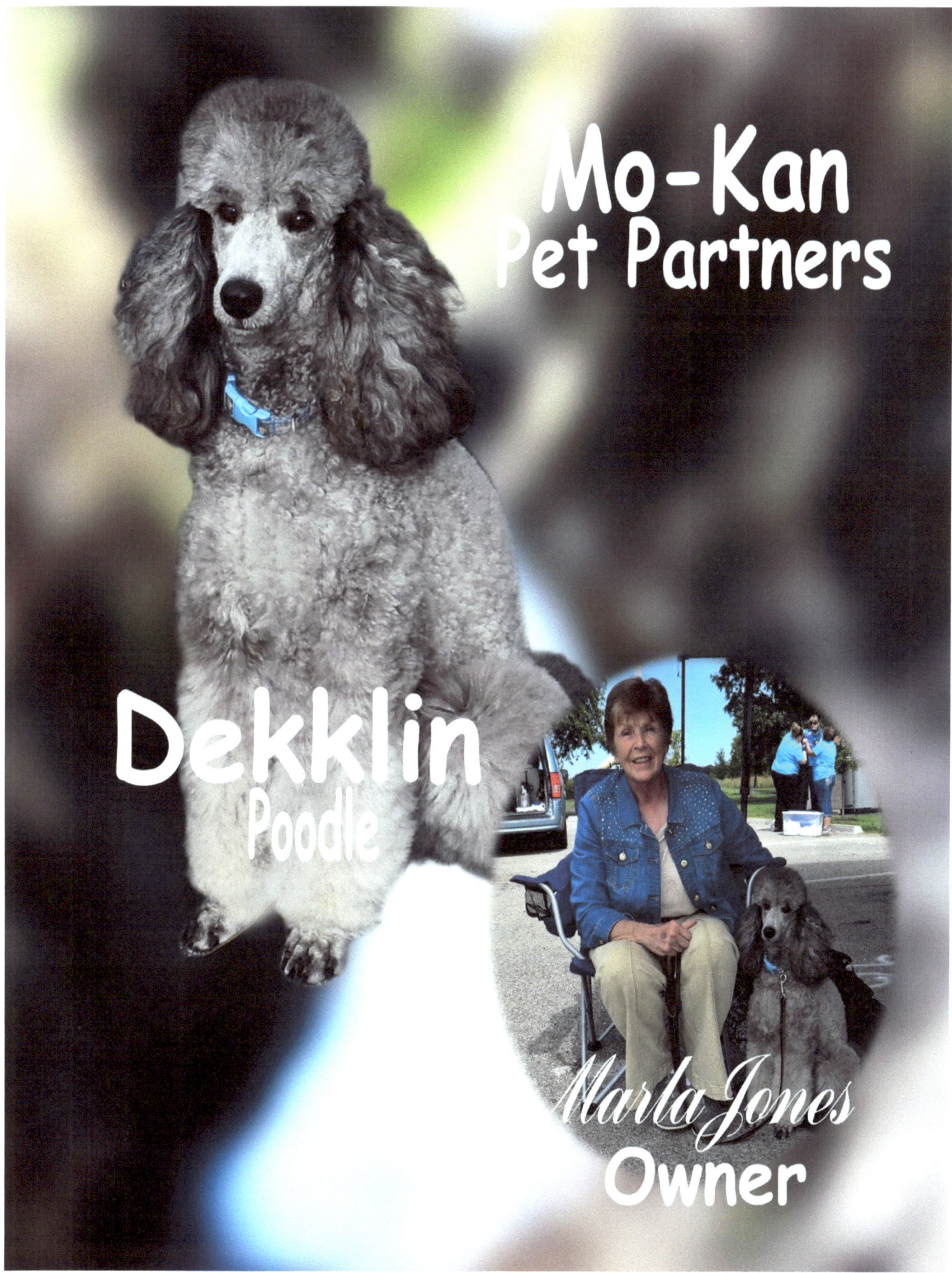

Mo-Kan
Pet Partners

Dekklin
Poodle

Marla Jones
Owner

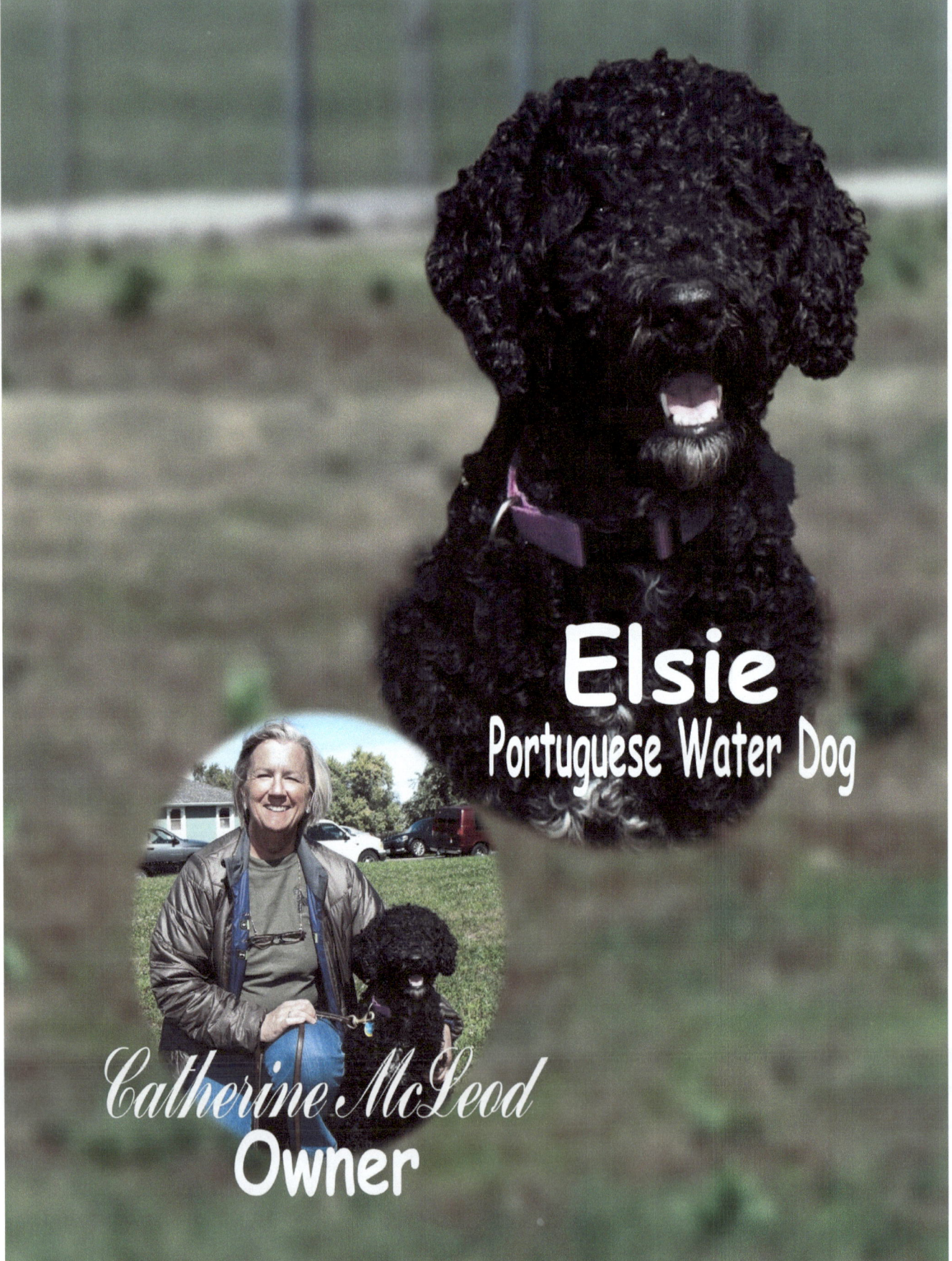

Elsie
Portuguese Water Dog

Catherine McLeod
Owner

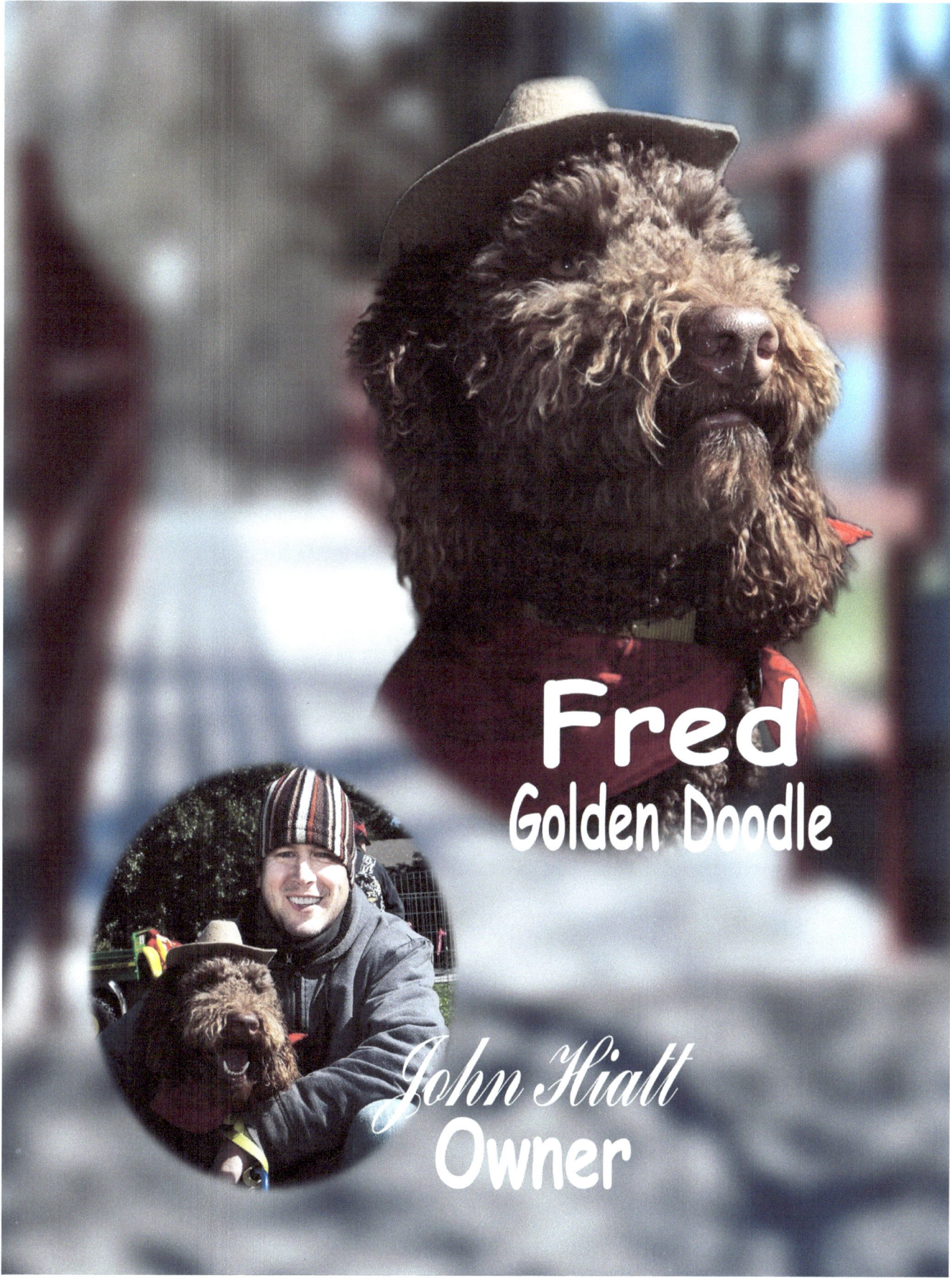

Fred
Golden Doodle

John Hiatt
Owner

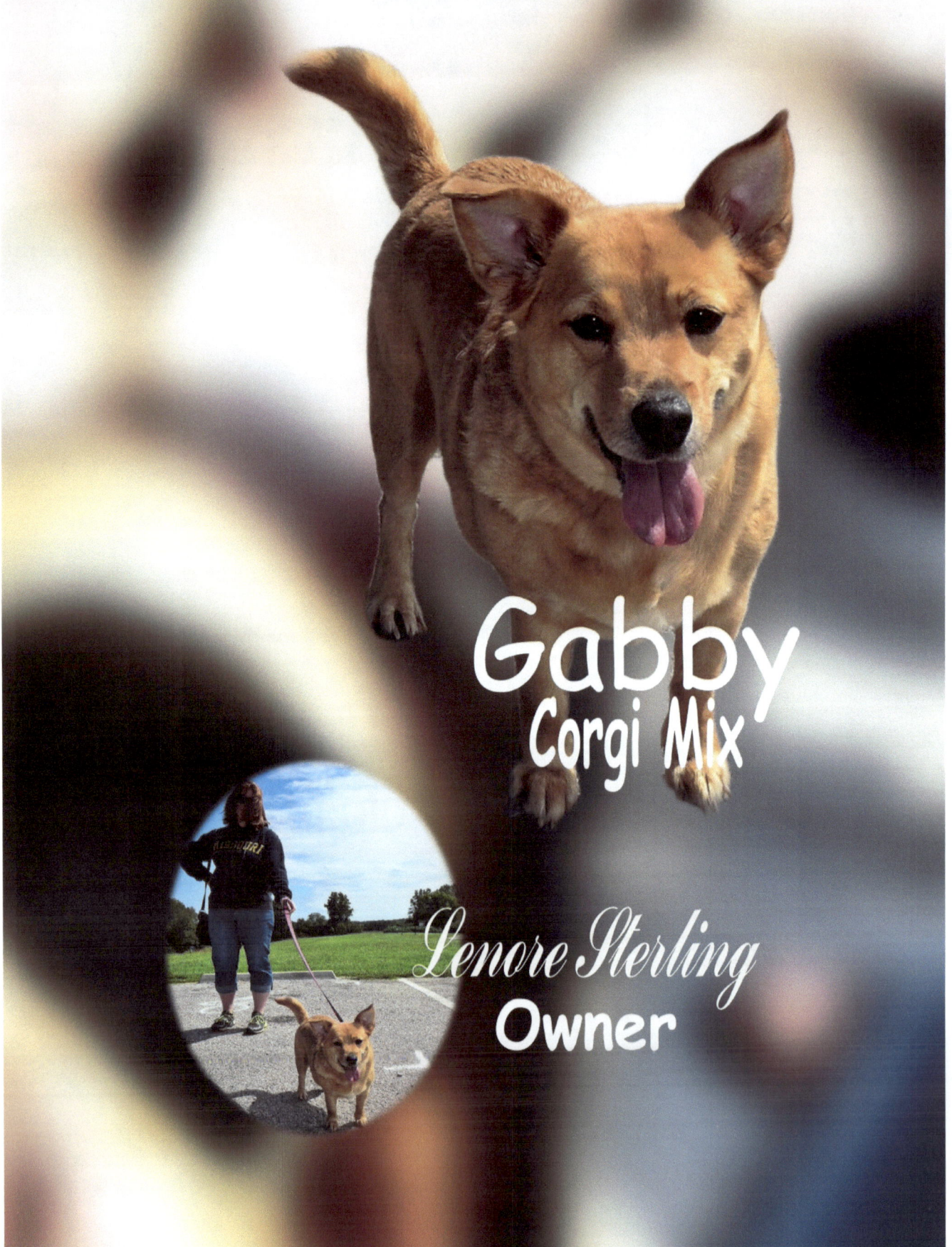

Gabby
Corgi Mix

Lenore Sterling
Owner

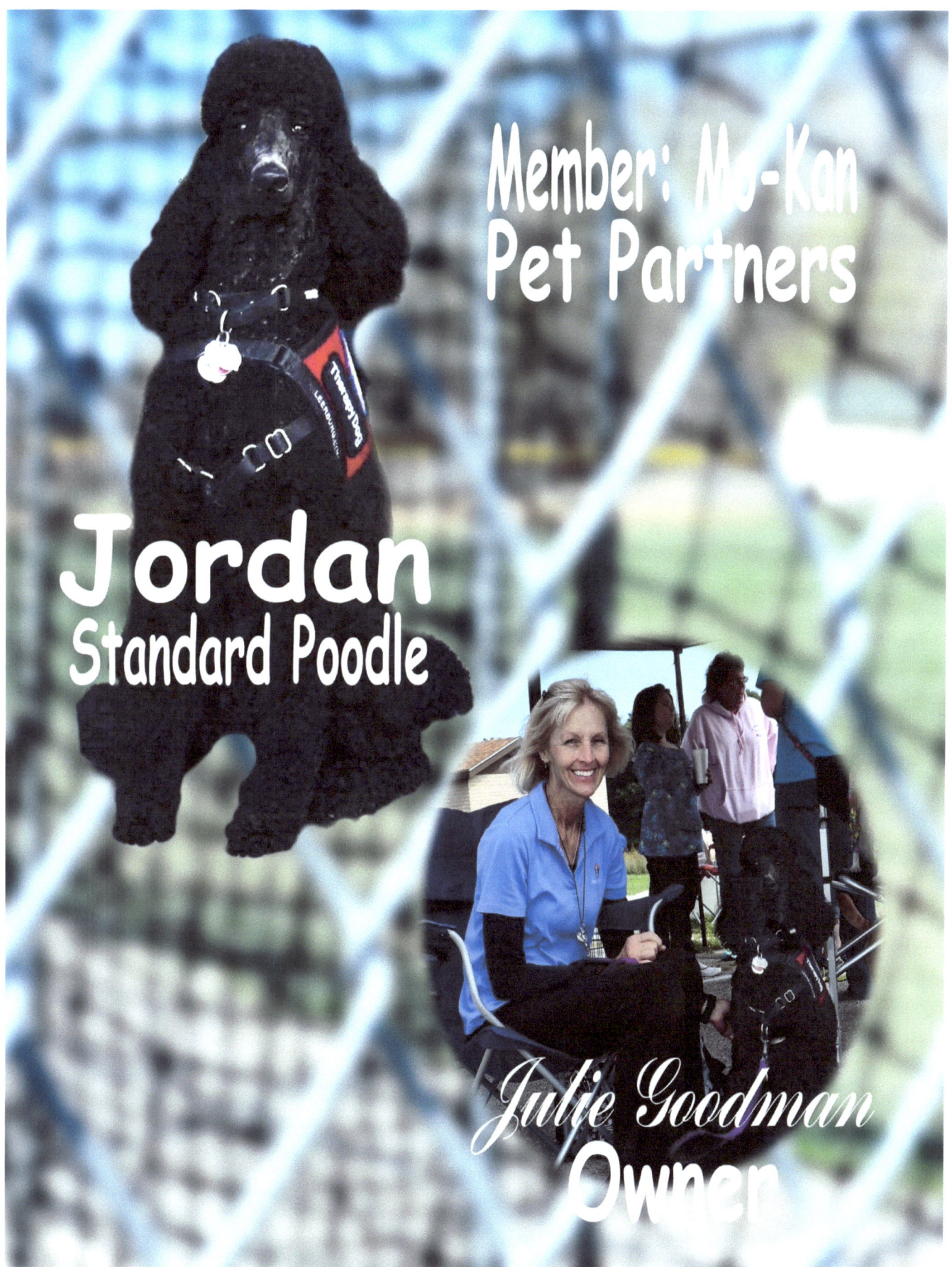

Member: Mo-Kan Pet Partners

Jordan
Standard Poodle

Julie Goodman
Owner

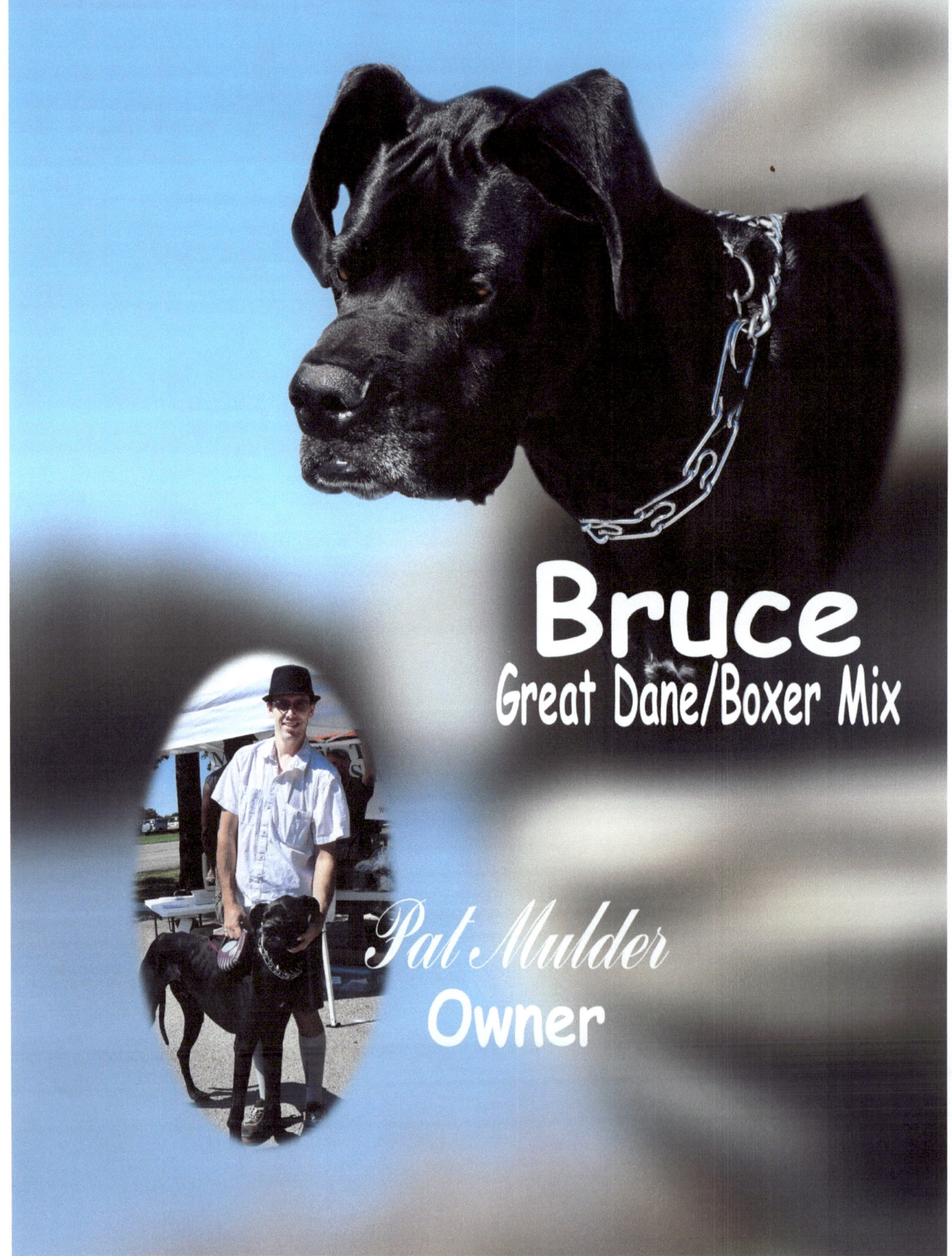

Bruce
Great Dane/Boxer Mix

Pat Mulder
Owner

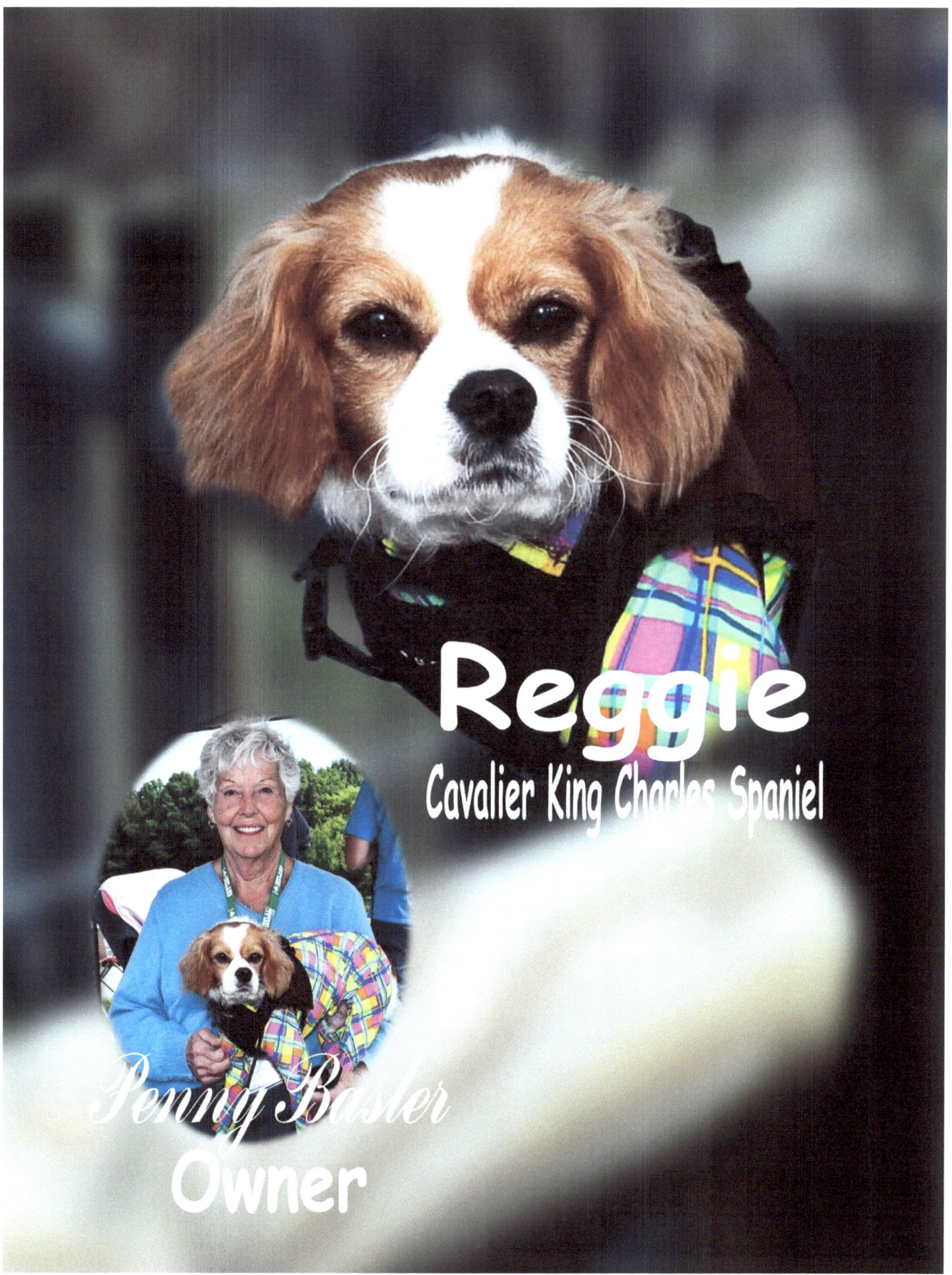

Reggie
Cavalier King Charles Spaniel

Penny Basler
Owner

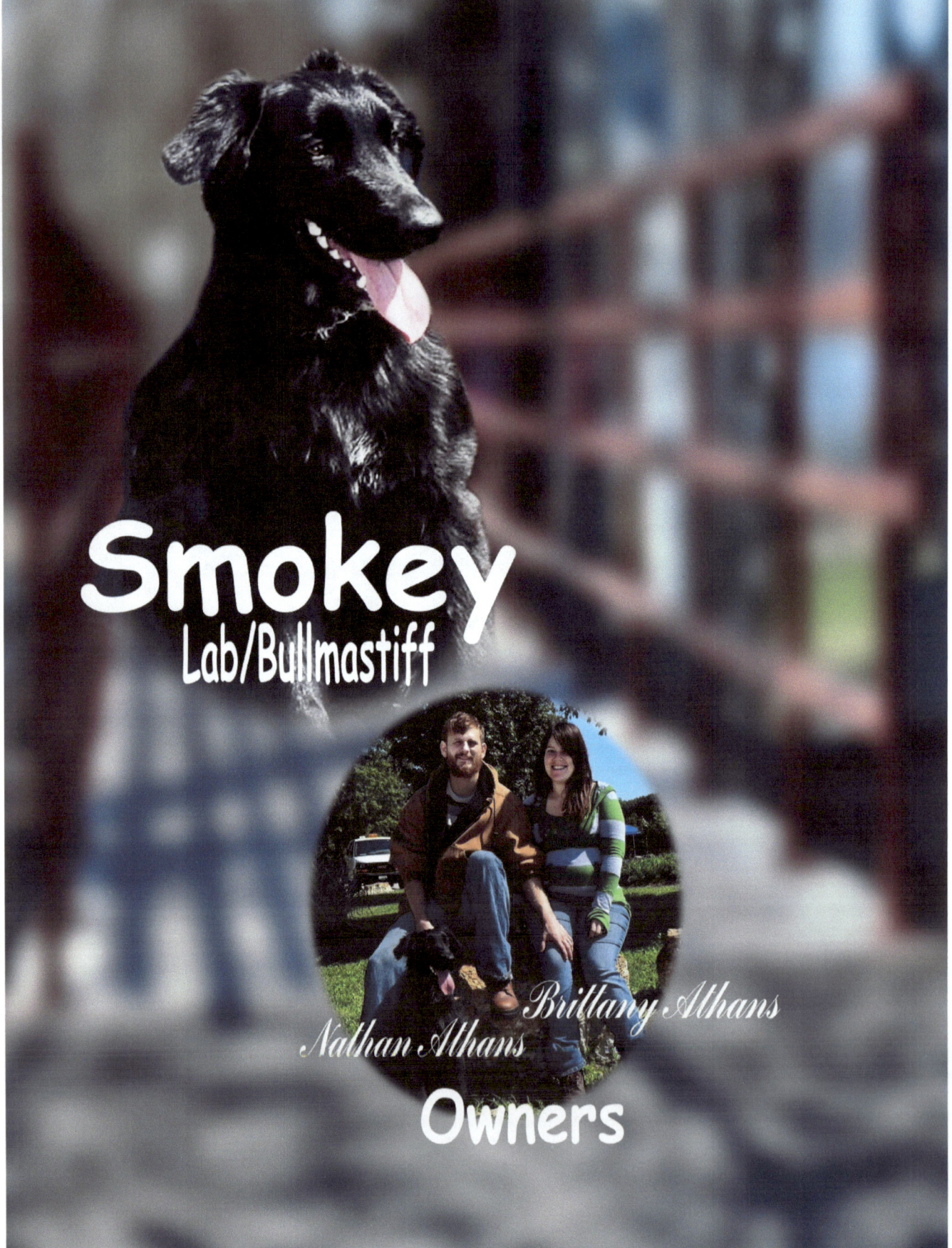

Smokey
Lab/Bullmastiff

Brittany Athans
Nathan Athans

Owners

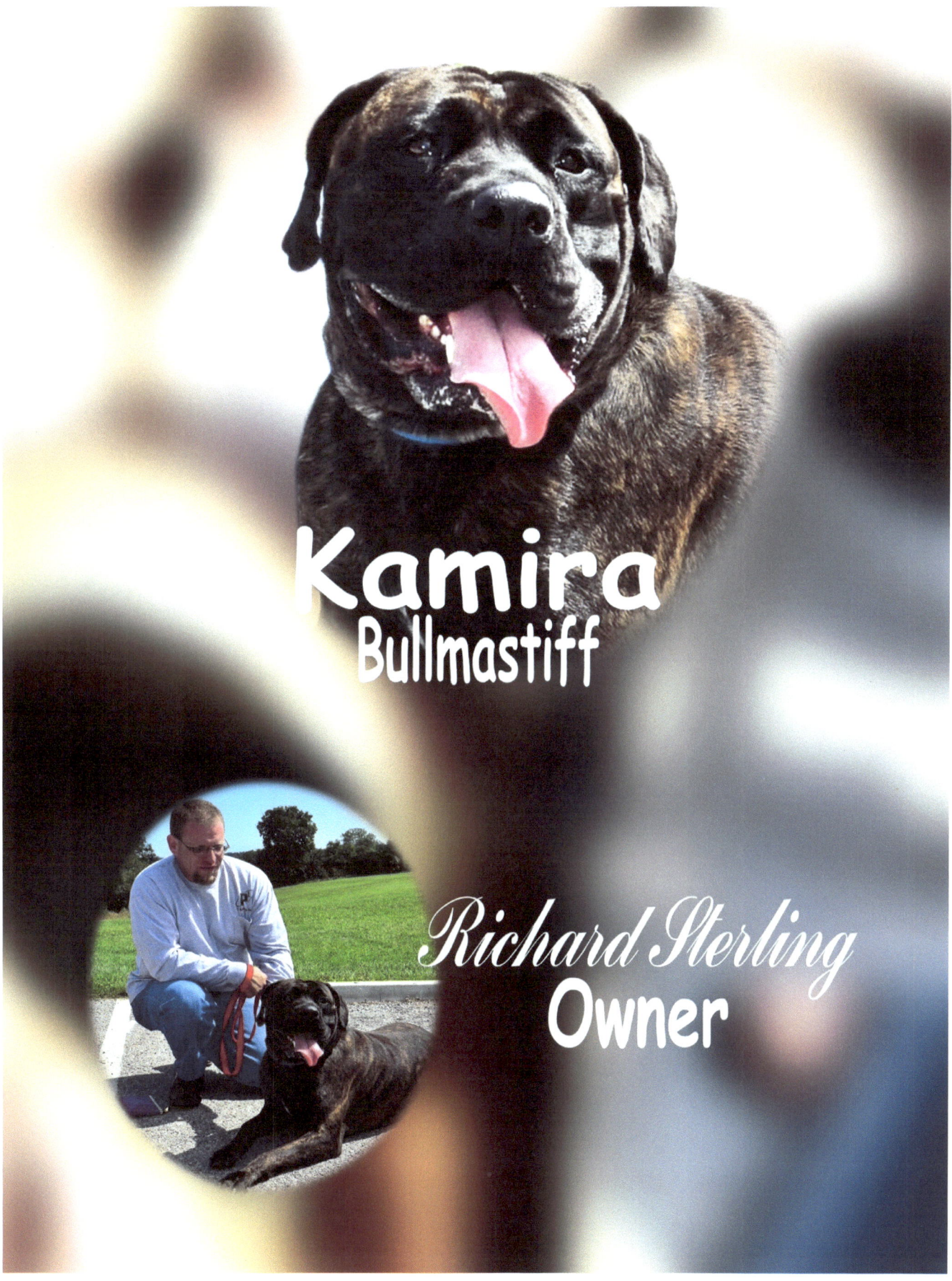

Kamira
Bullmastiff

Richard Sterling
Owner

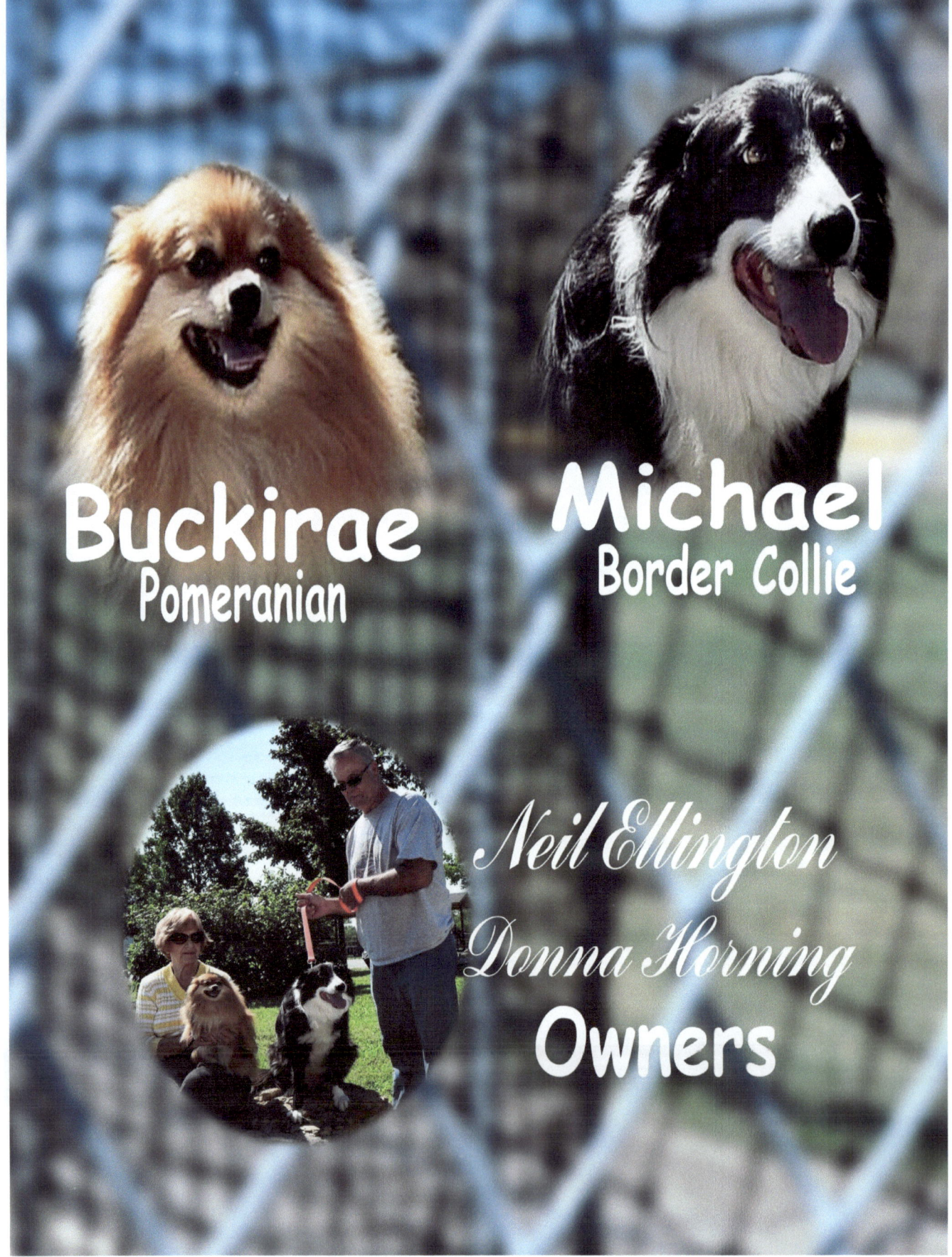

Buckirae
Pomeranian

Michael
Border Collie

Neil Ellington

Donna Horning
Owners

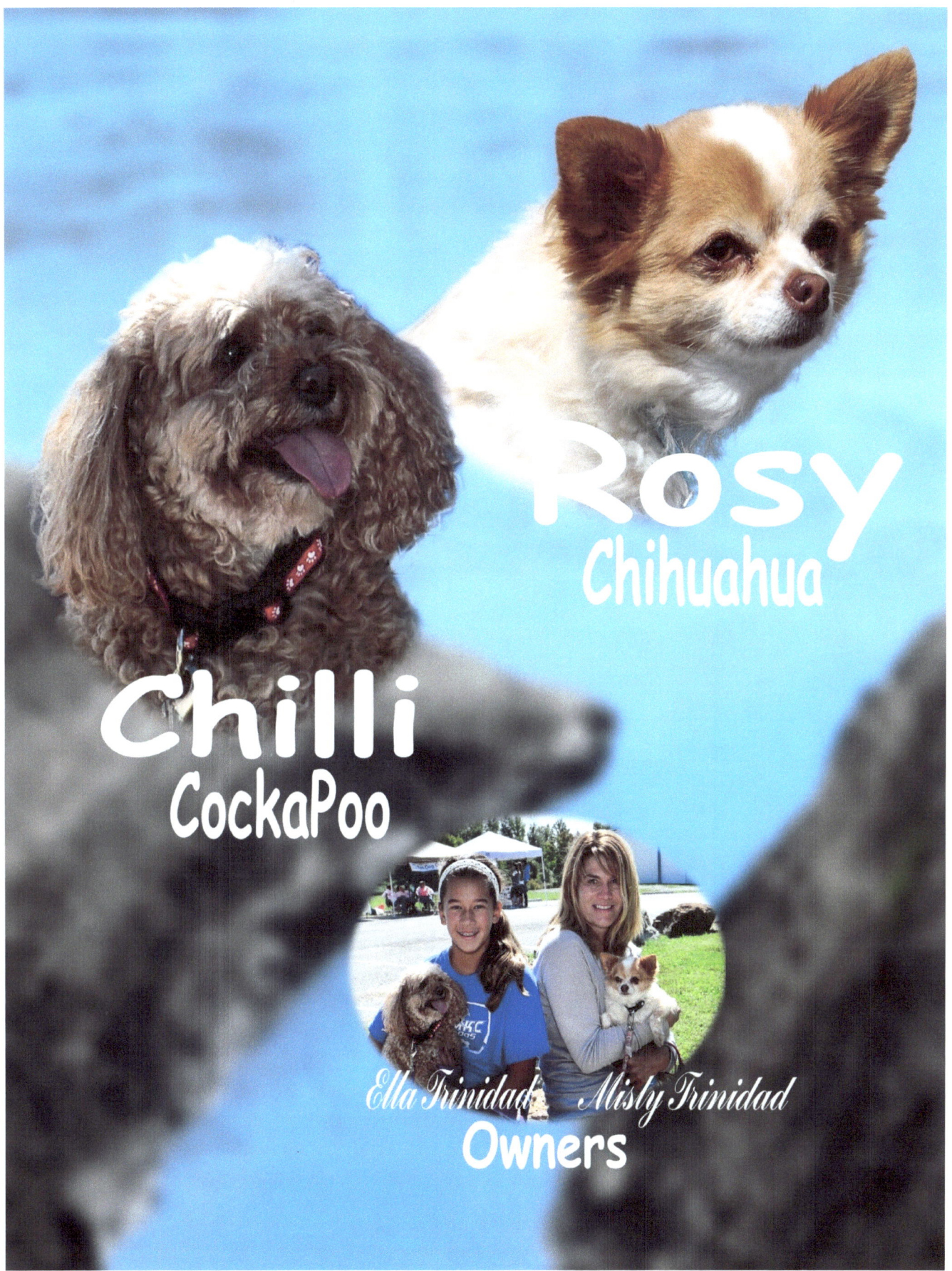

Rosy
Chihuahua

Chilli
CockaPoo

Ella Trinidad   Misty Trinidad
Owners

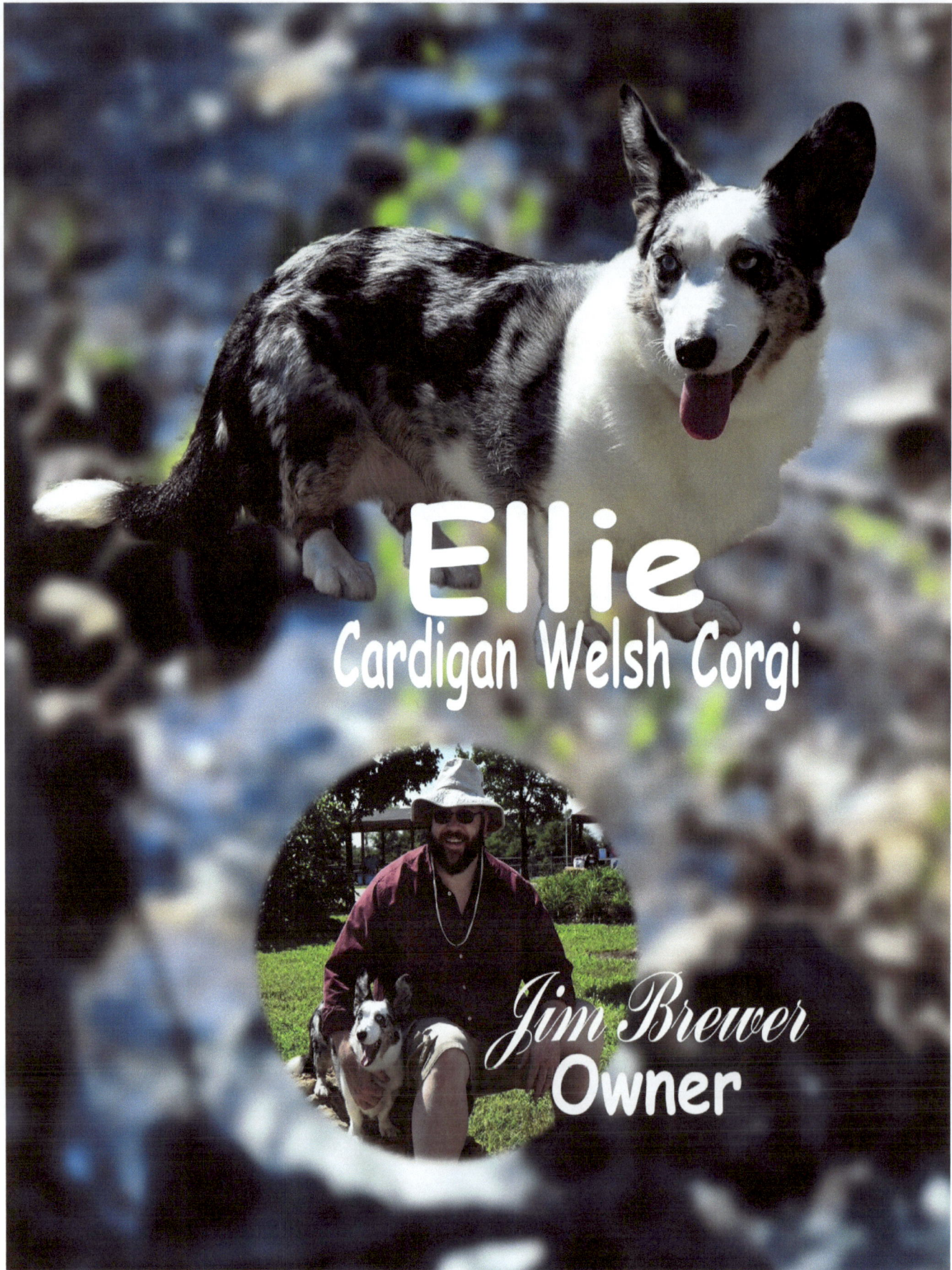

Ellie
Cardigan Welsh Corgi

Jim Brewer
Owner

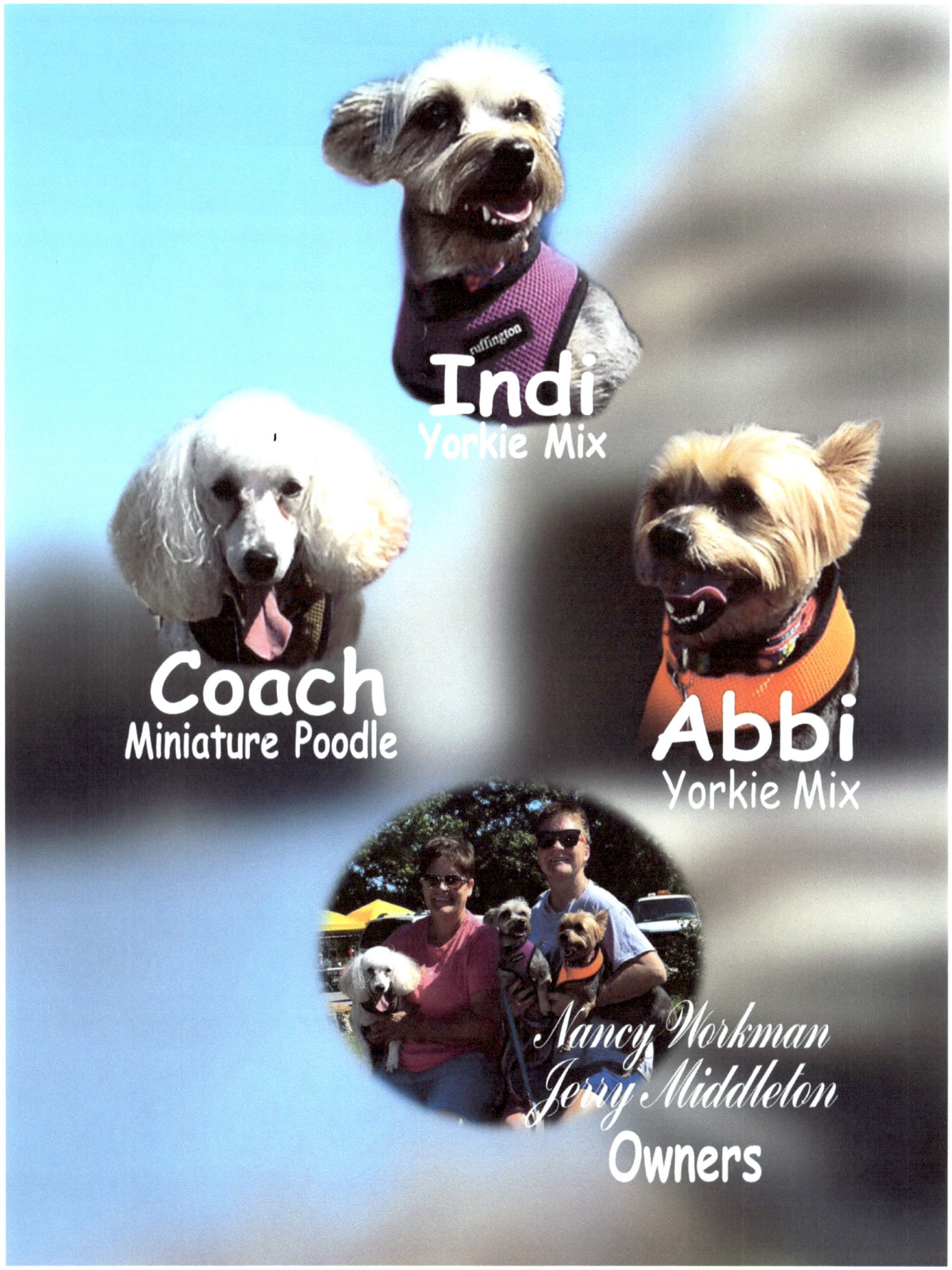

Indi
Yorkie Mix

Coach
Miniature Poodle

Abbi
Yorkie Mix

Nancy Workman
Jerry Middleton
Owners

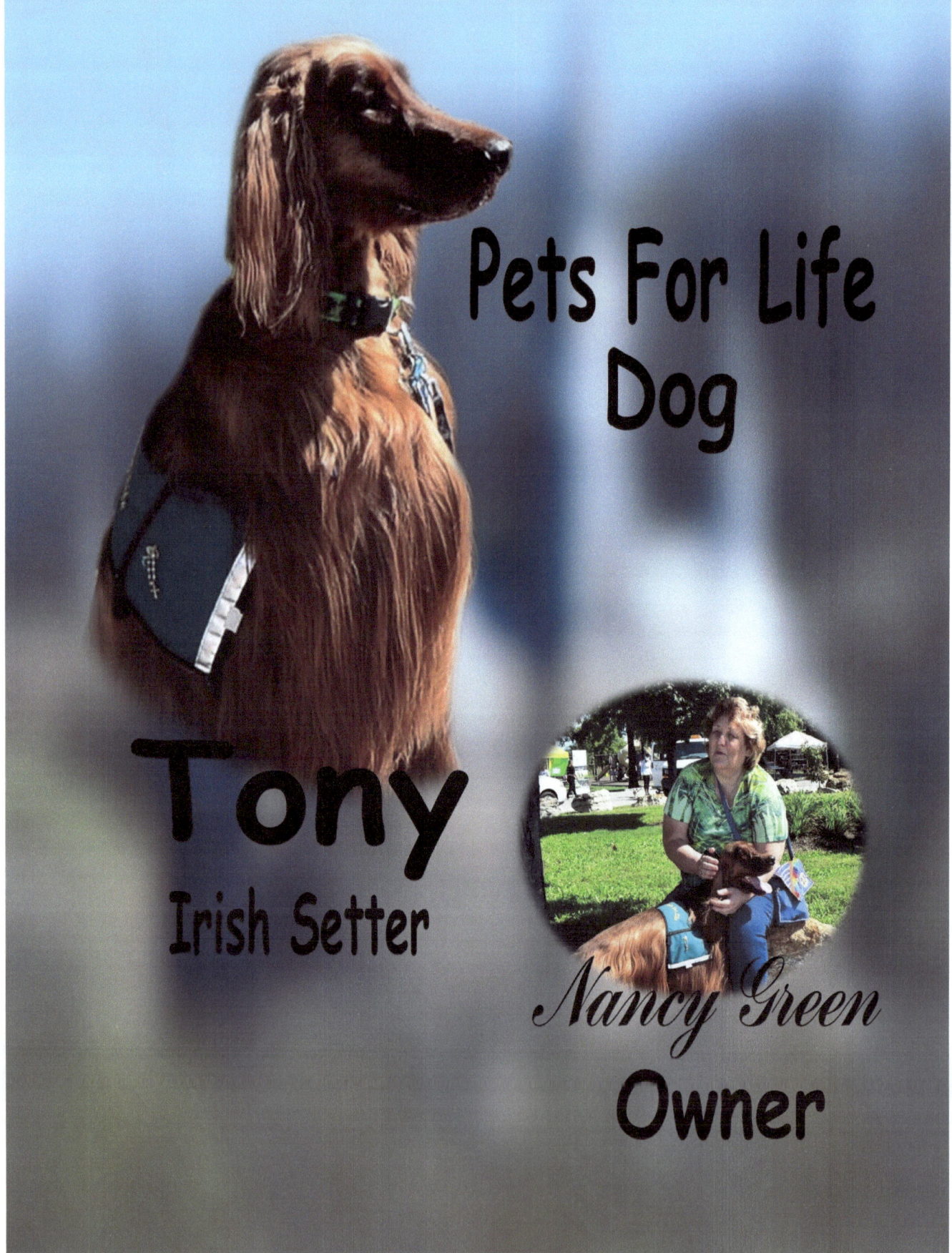

Pets For Life
Dog

Tony
Irish Setter

Nancy Green
Owner

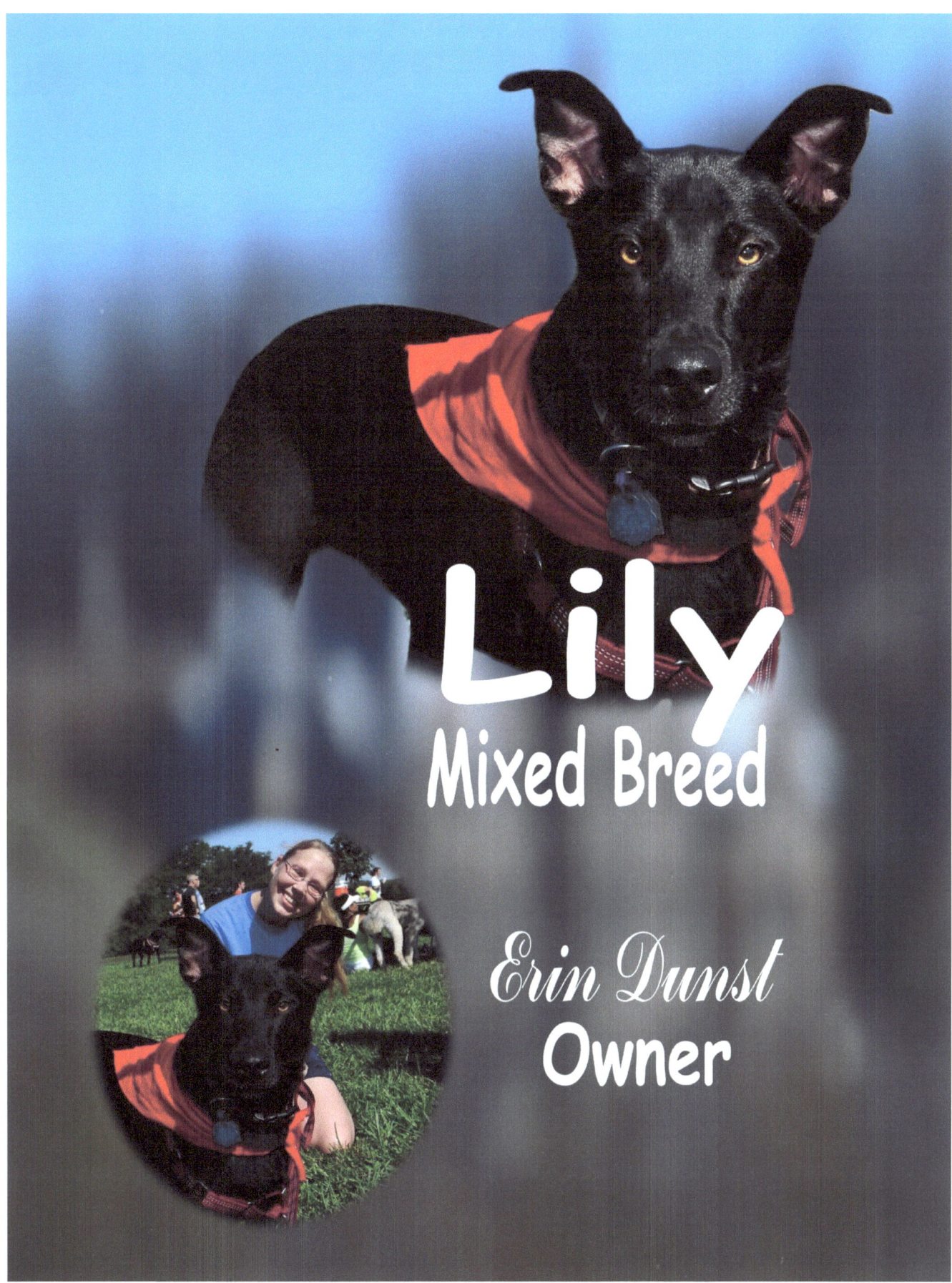

Lily
Mixed Breed

Erin Dunst
Owner

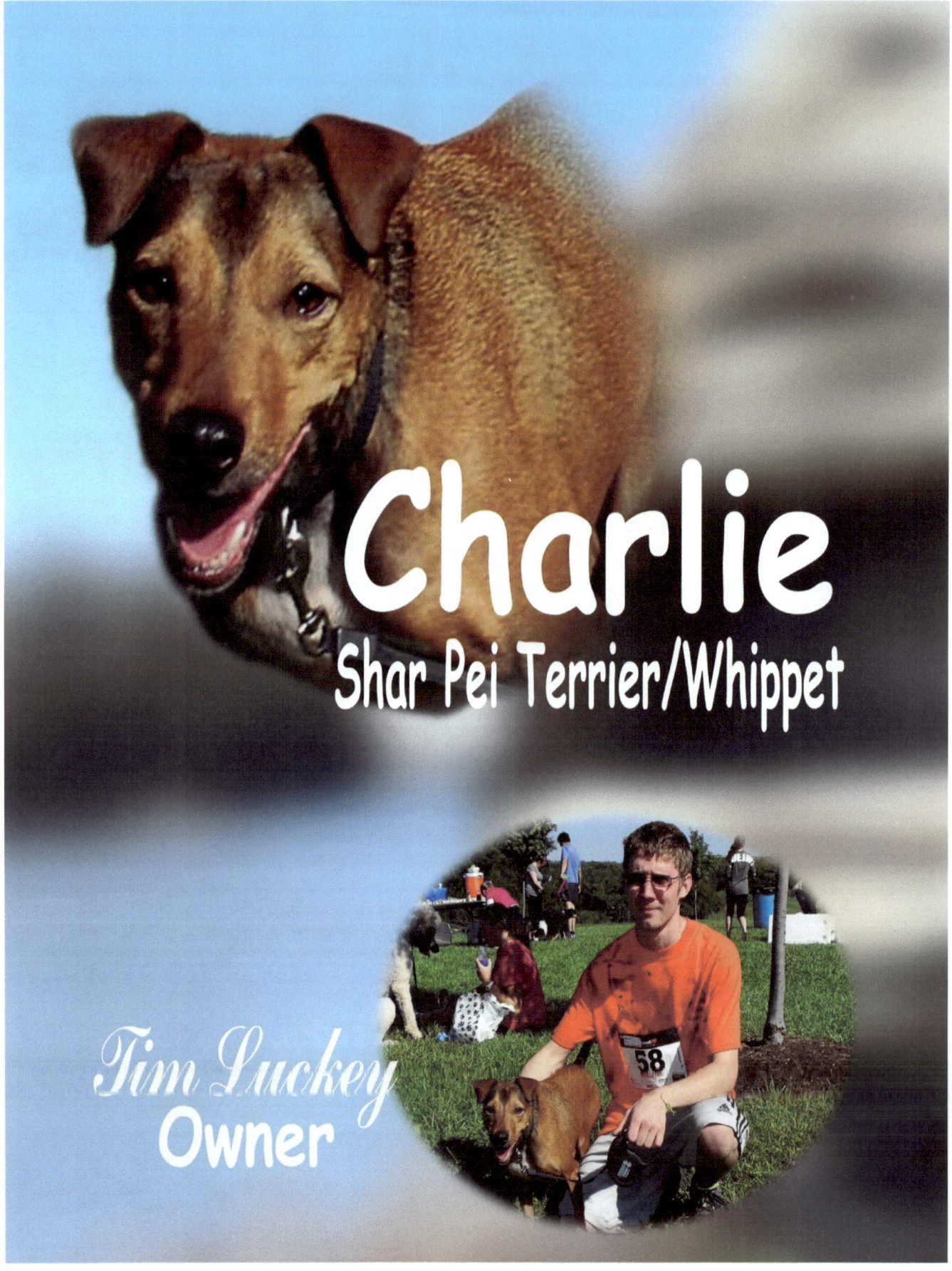

Charlie
Shar Pei Terrier/Whippet

Tim Luckey
Owner

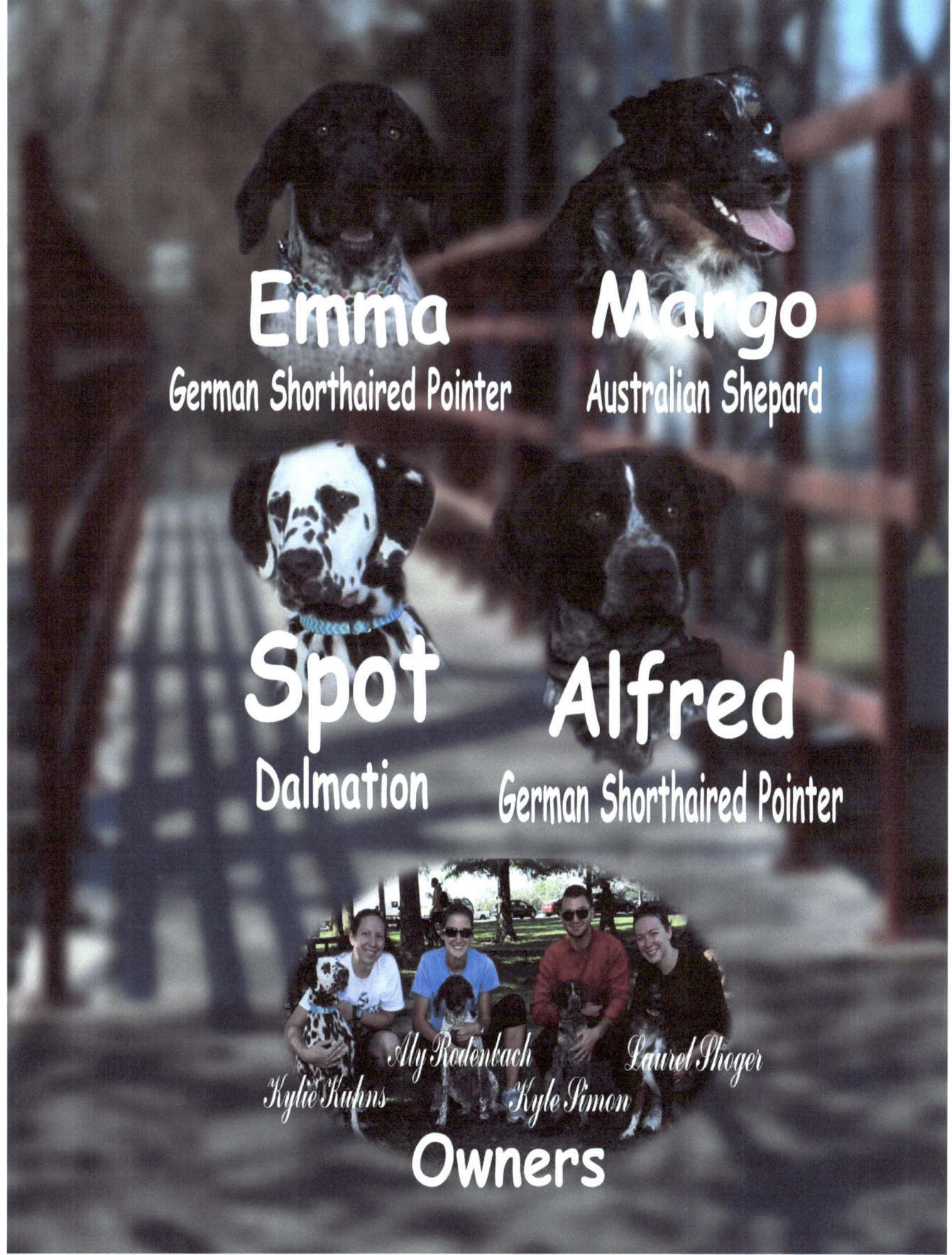

Emma
German Shorthaired Pointer

Margo
Australian Shepard

Spot
Dalmation

Alfred
German Shorthaired Pointer

Kylie Kuhns Aly Rodenbach Kyle Simon Laurel Shoger

Owners

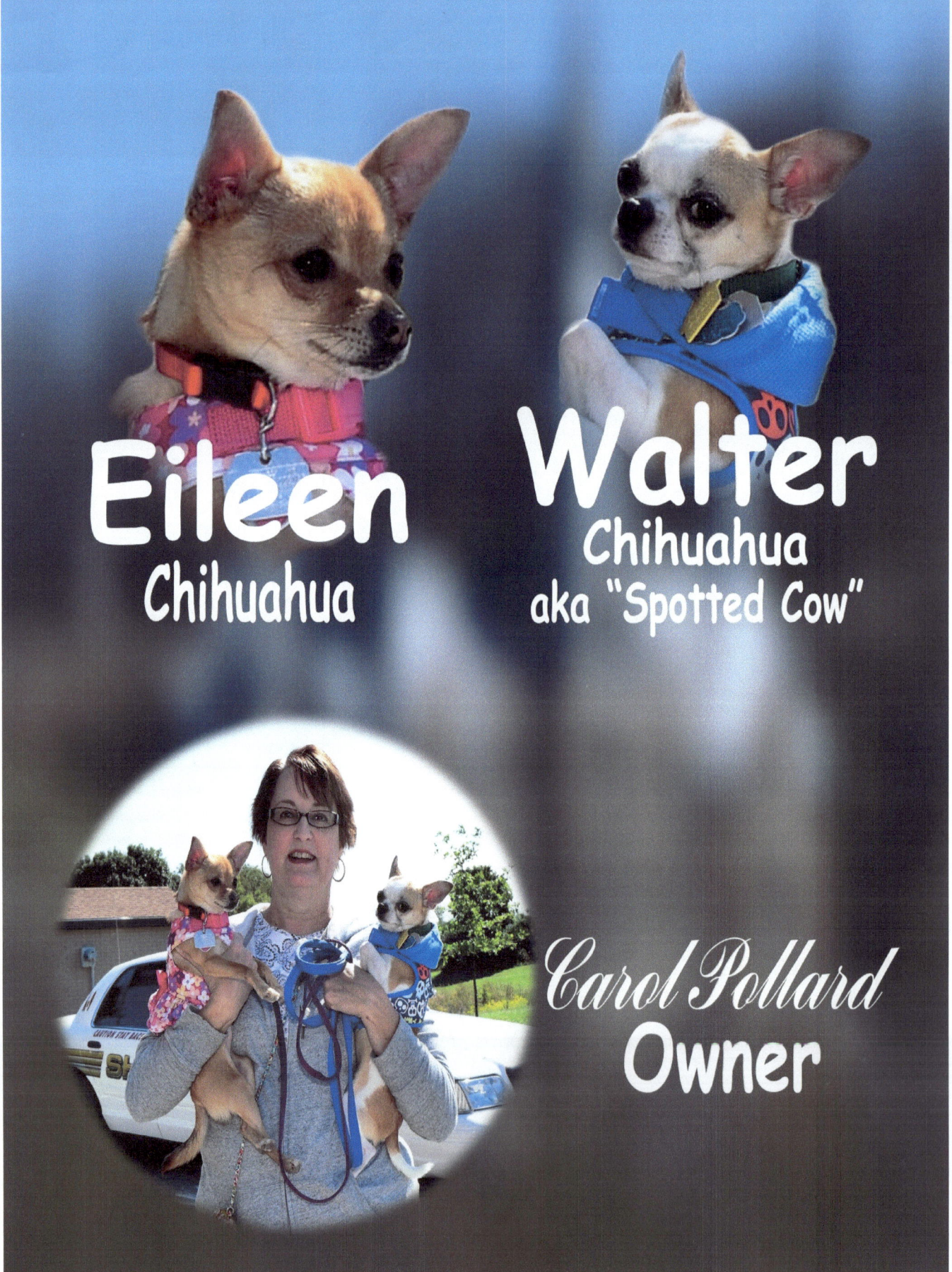

Eileen
Chihuahua

Walter
Chihuahua
aka "Spotted Cow"

Carol Pollard
Owner

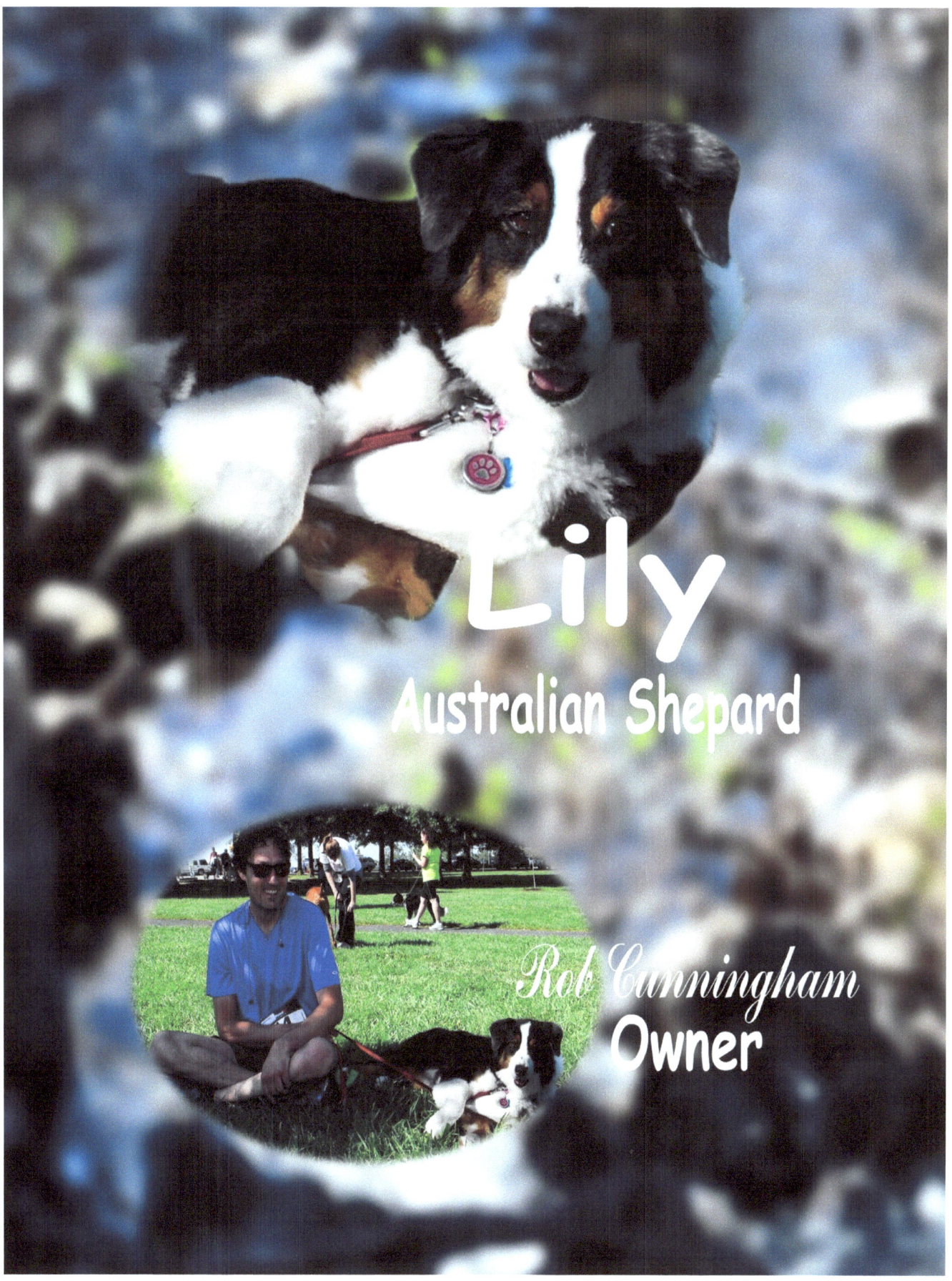

Lily
Australian Shepard

Rob Cunningham
Owner

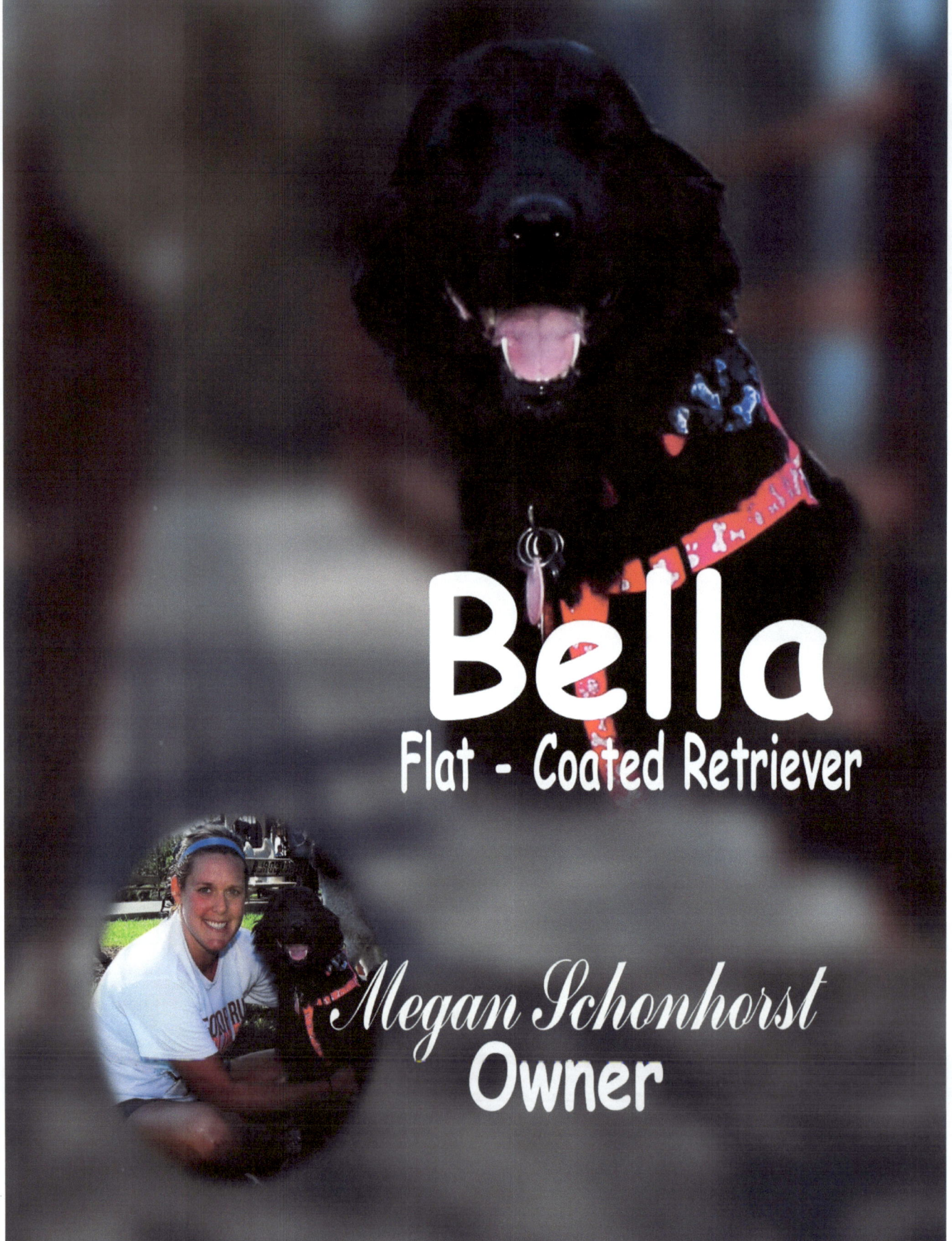

Bella
Flat - Coated Retriever

Megan Schonhorst
Owner

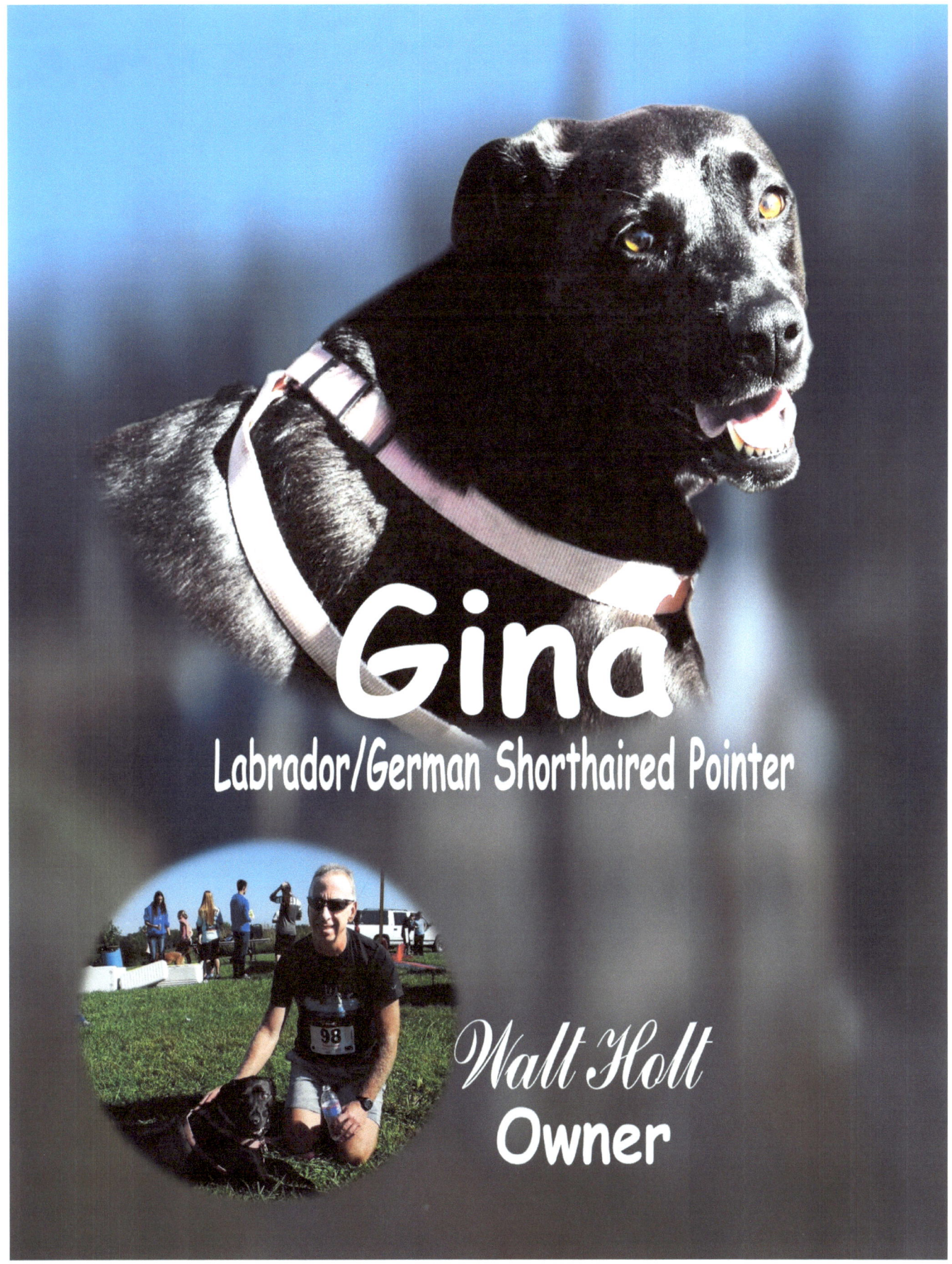

Gina
Labrador/German Shorthaired Pointer

Walt Holt
Owner

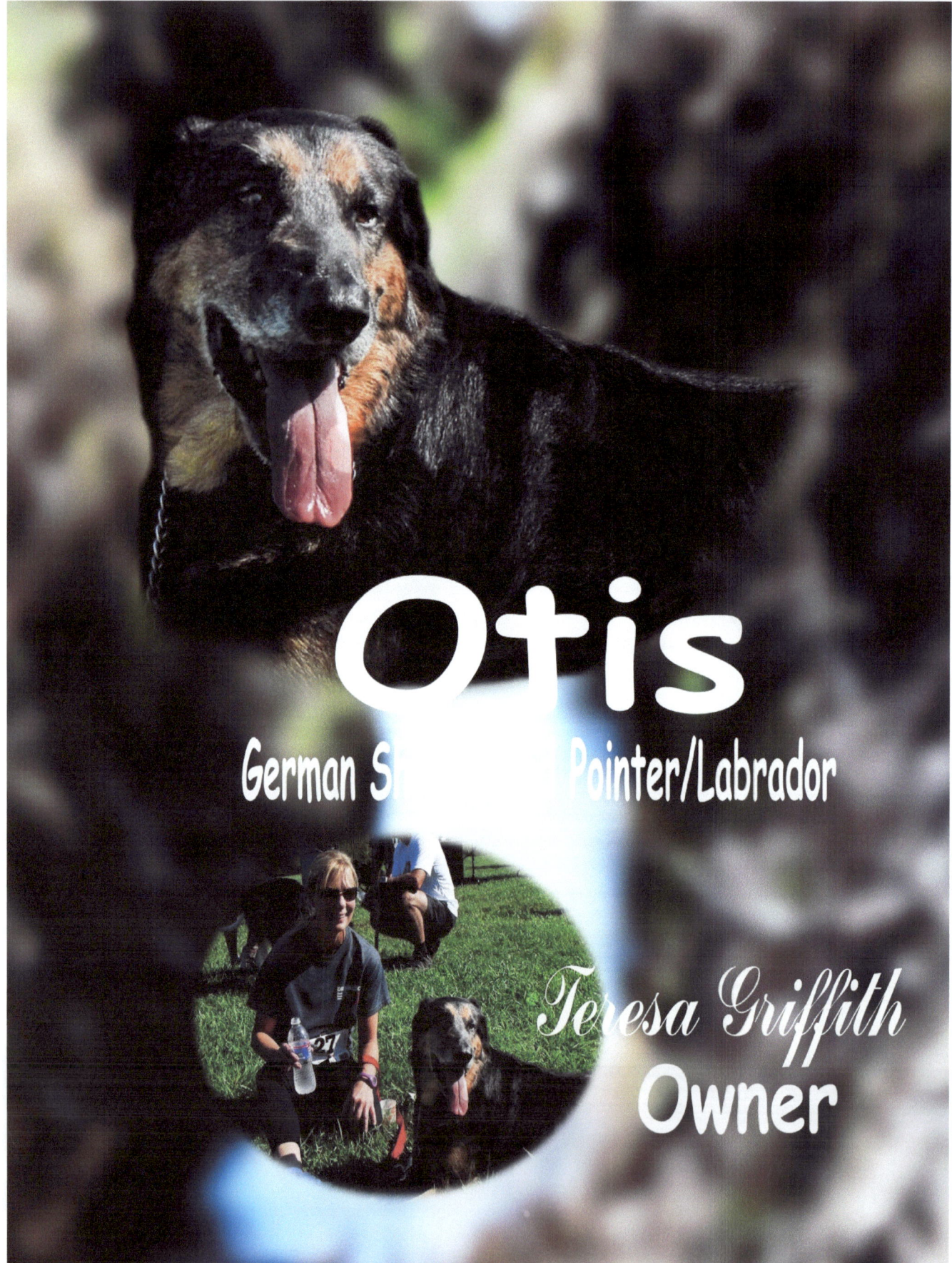

Otis

German Shorthaired Pointer/Labrador

Teresa Griffith
Owner

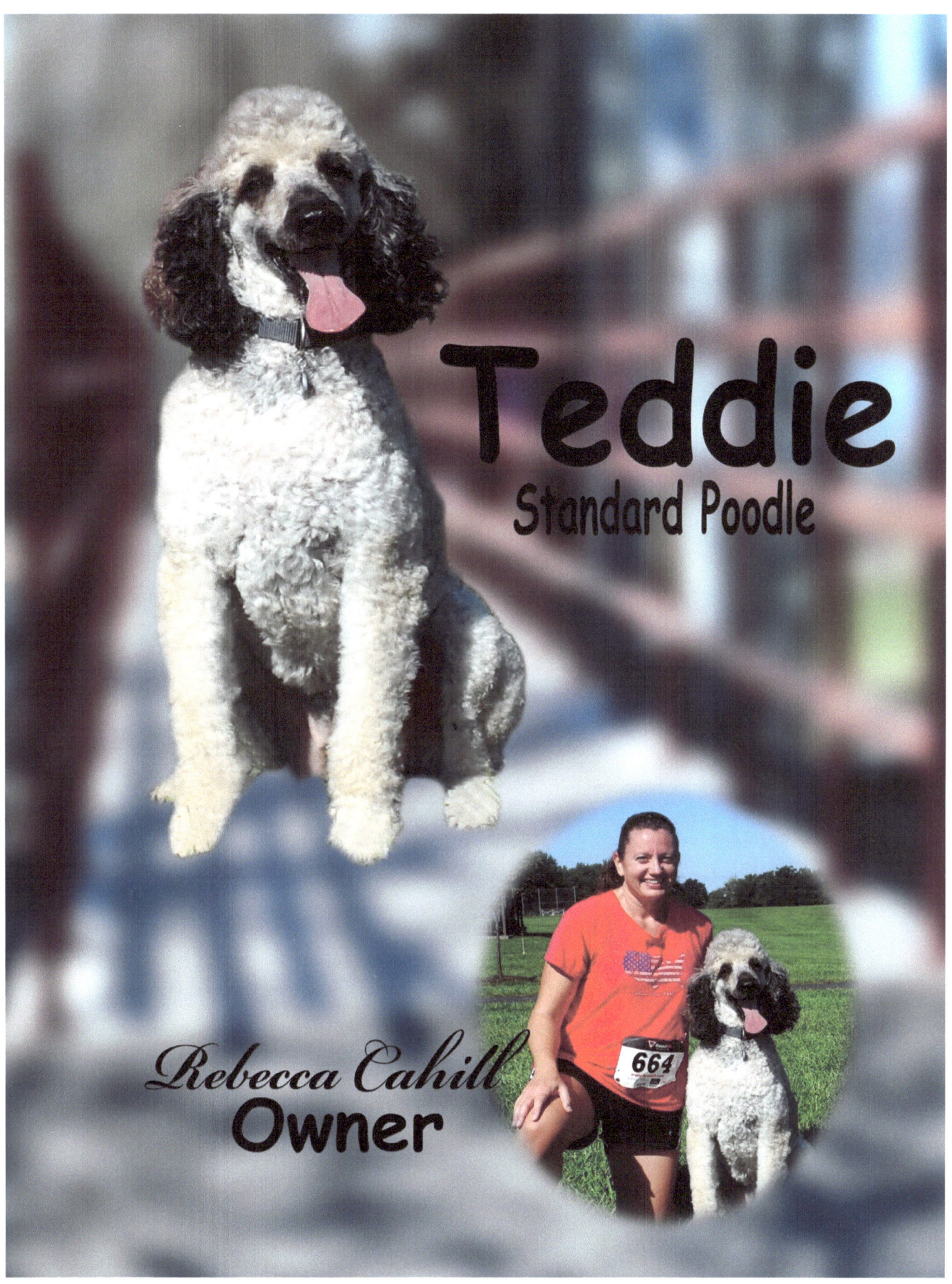

Teddie
Standard Poodle

Rebecca Cahill
Owner

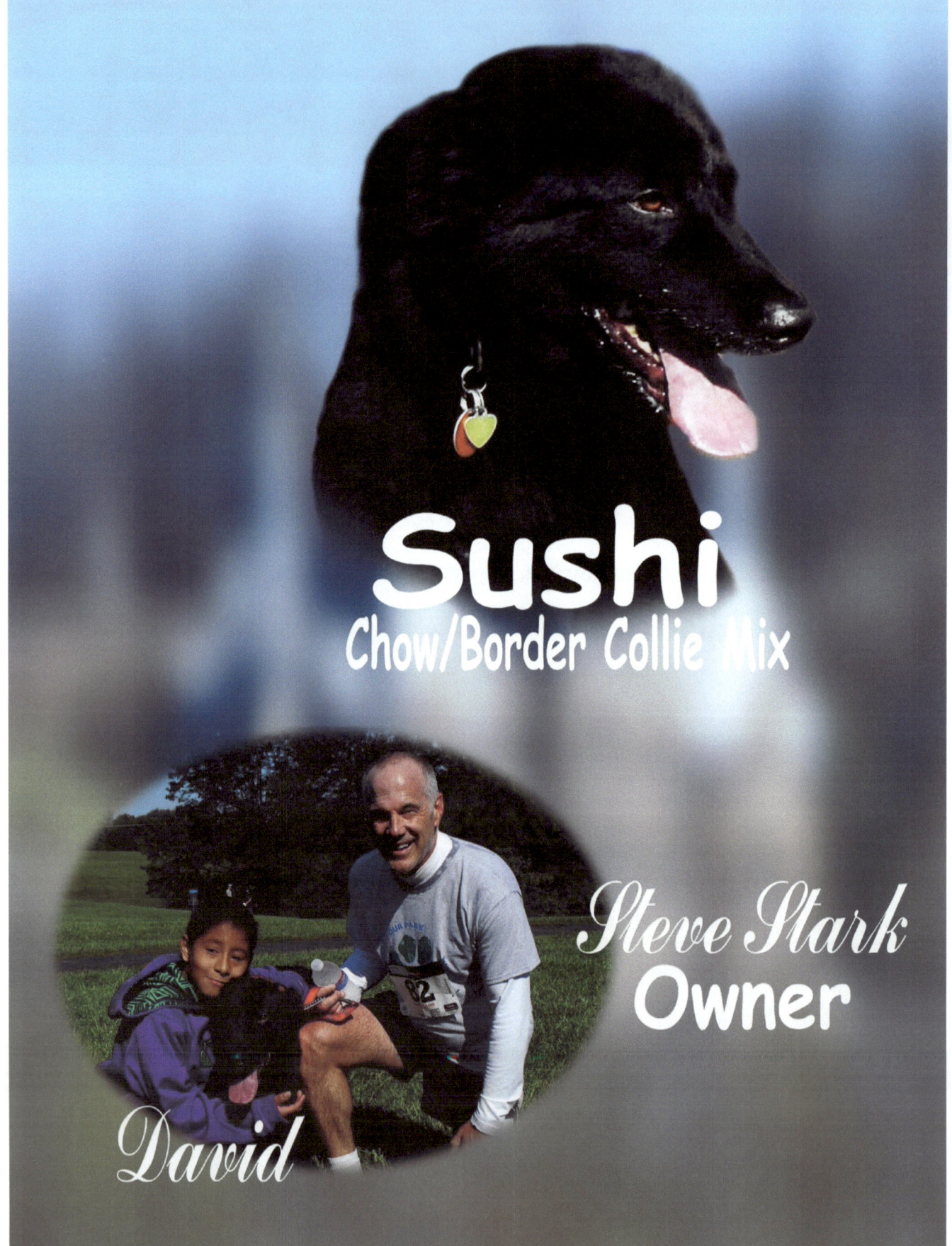

Sushi
Chow/Border Collie Mix

Steve Stark
Owner

David

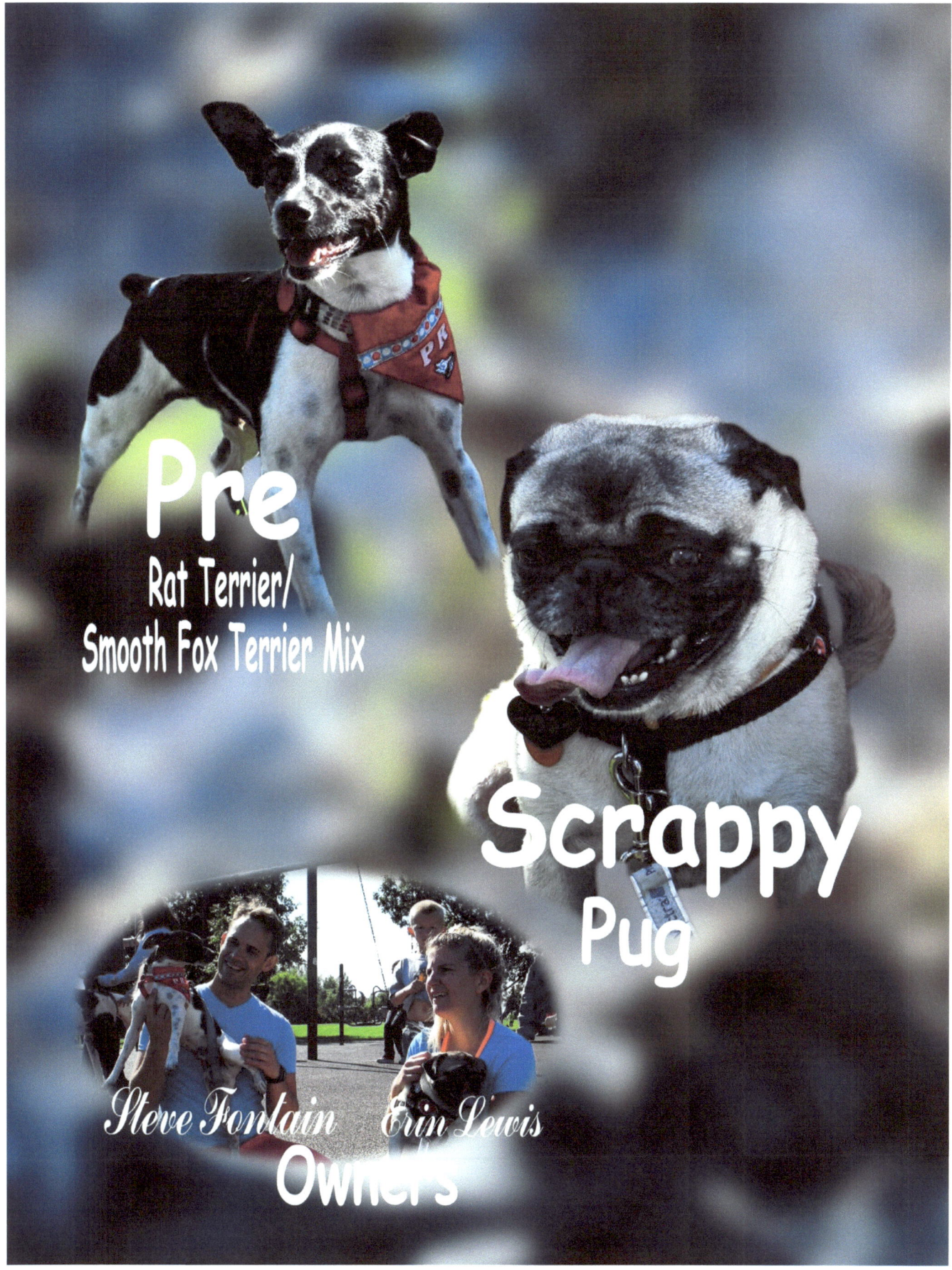

Pre
Rat Terrier/
Smooth Fox Terrier Mix

Scrappy
Pug

Steve Fontain   Erin Lewis
Owners

Skydeck Publishing

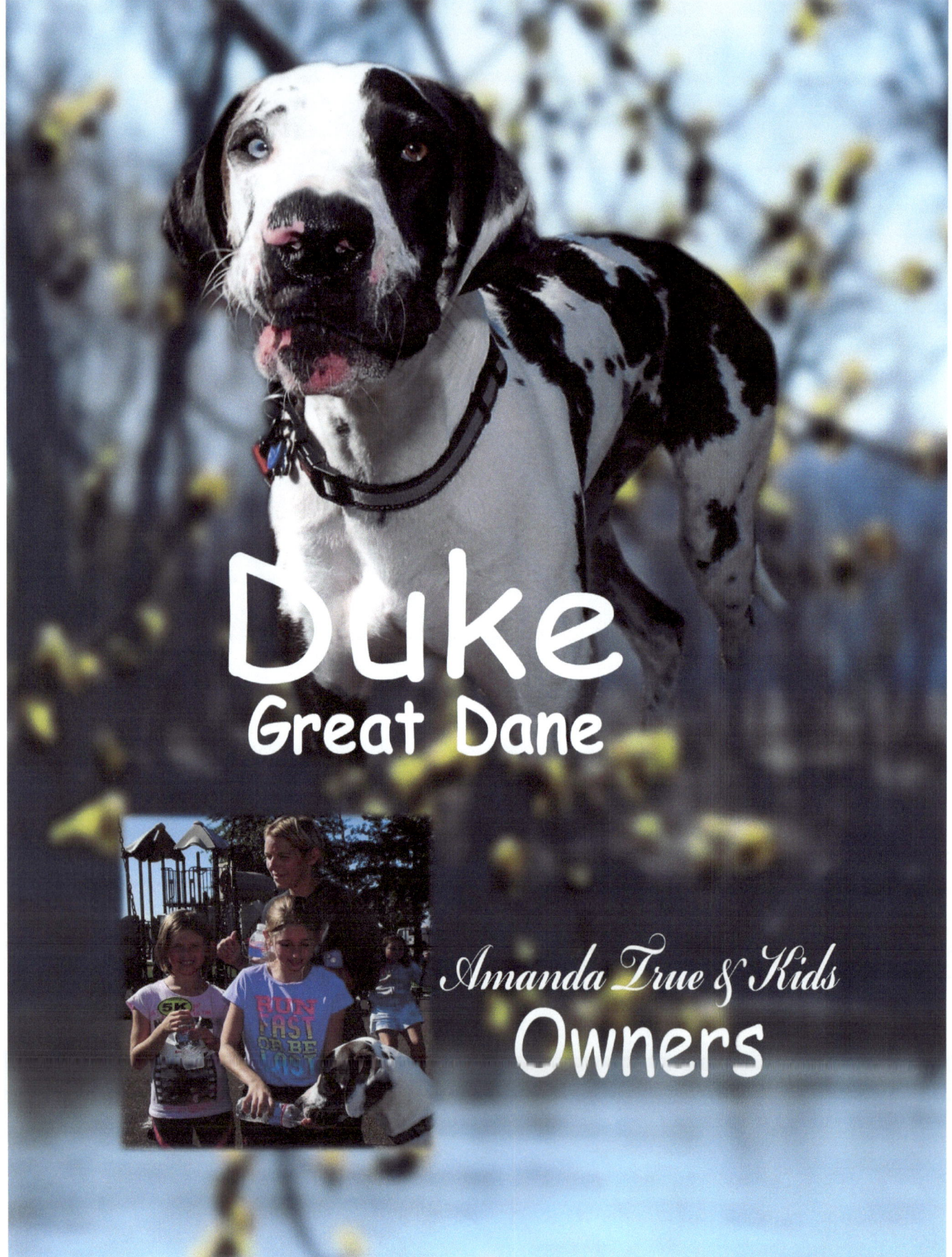

Duke
Great Dane

Amanda True & Kids
Owners

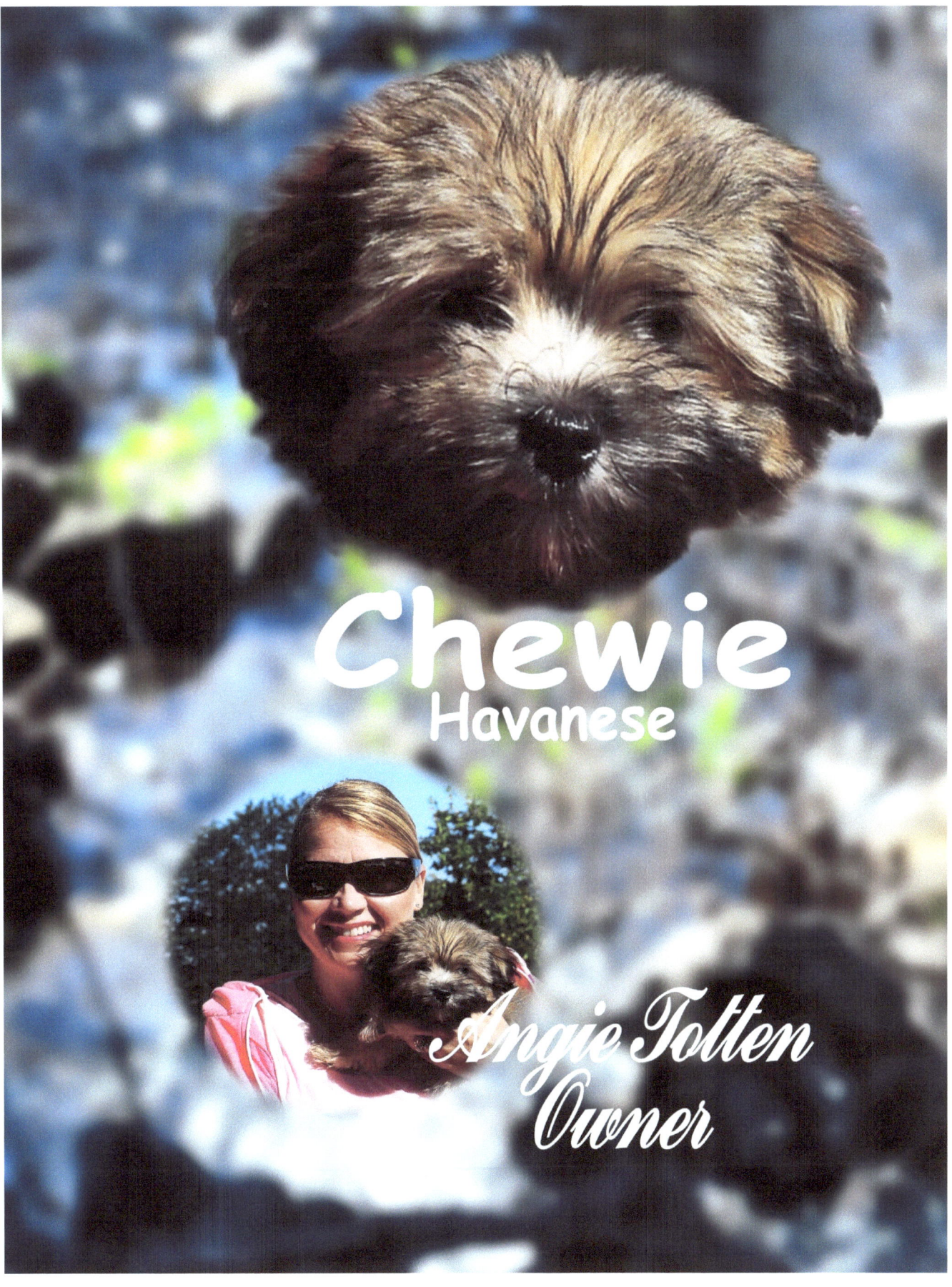

Chewie
Havanese

Angie Totten
Owner

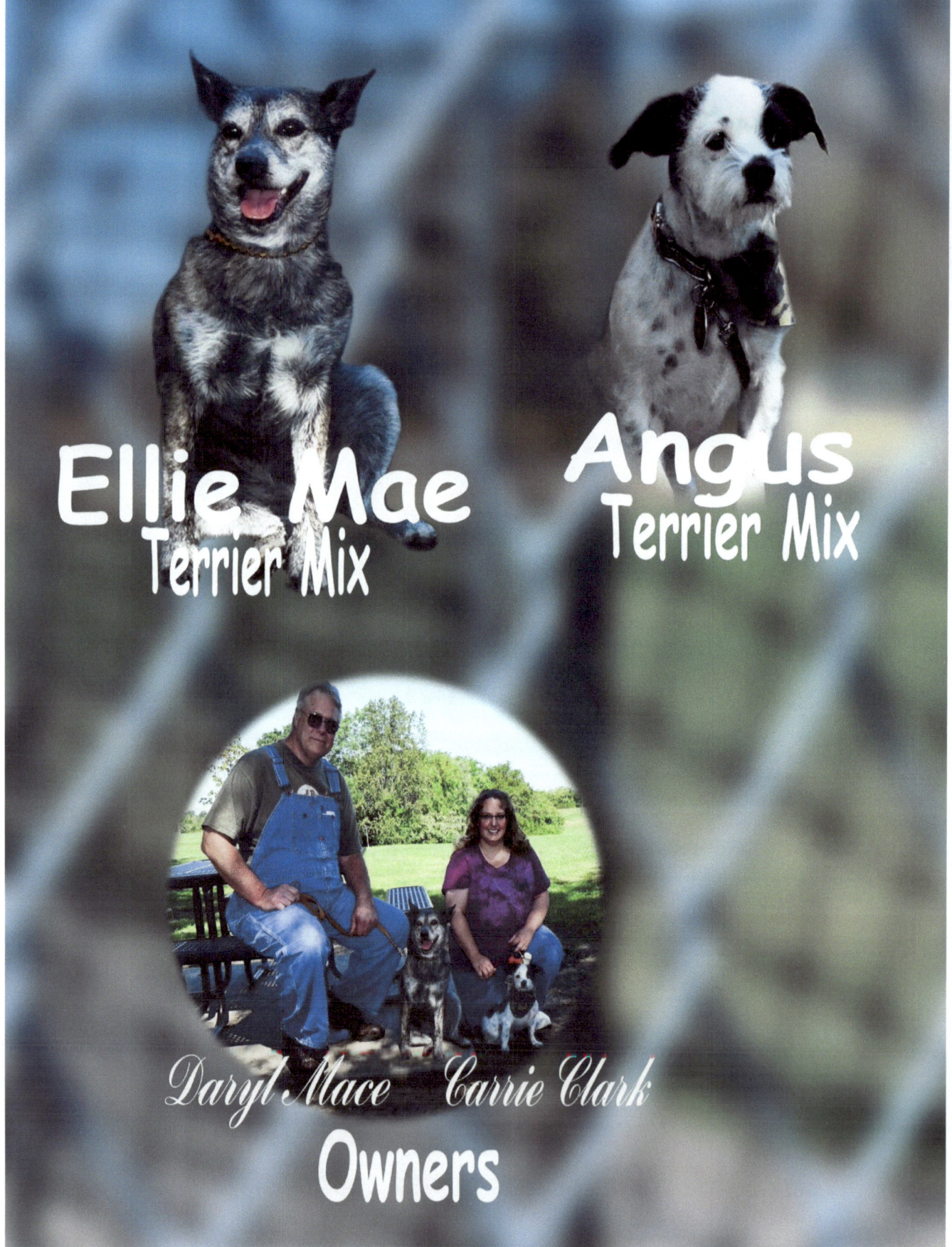

Ellie Mae
Terrier Mix

Angus
Terrier Mix

Daryl Mace   Carrie Clark
Owners

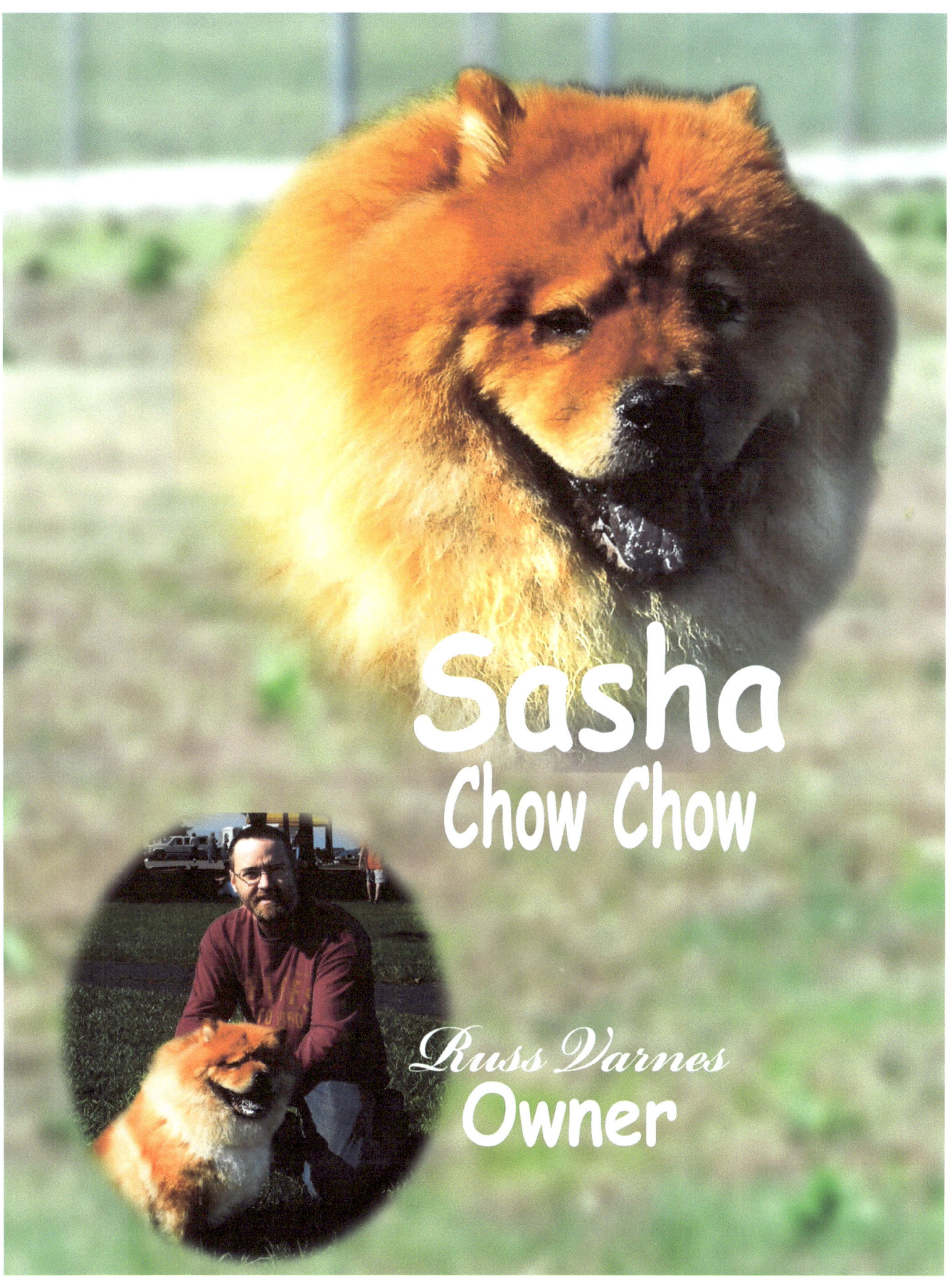

Sasha
Chow Chow

Russ Varnes
Owner

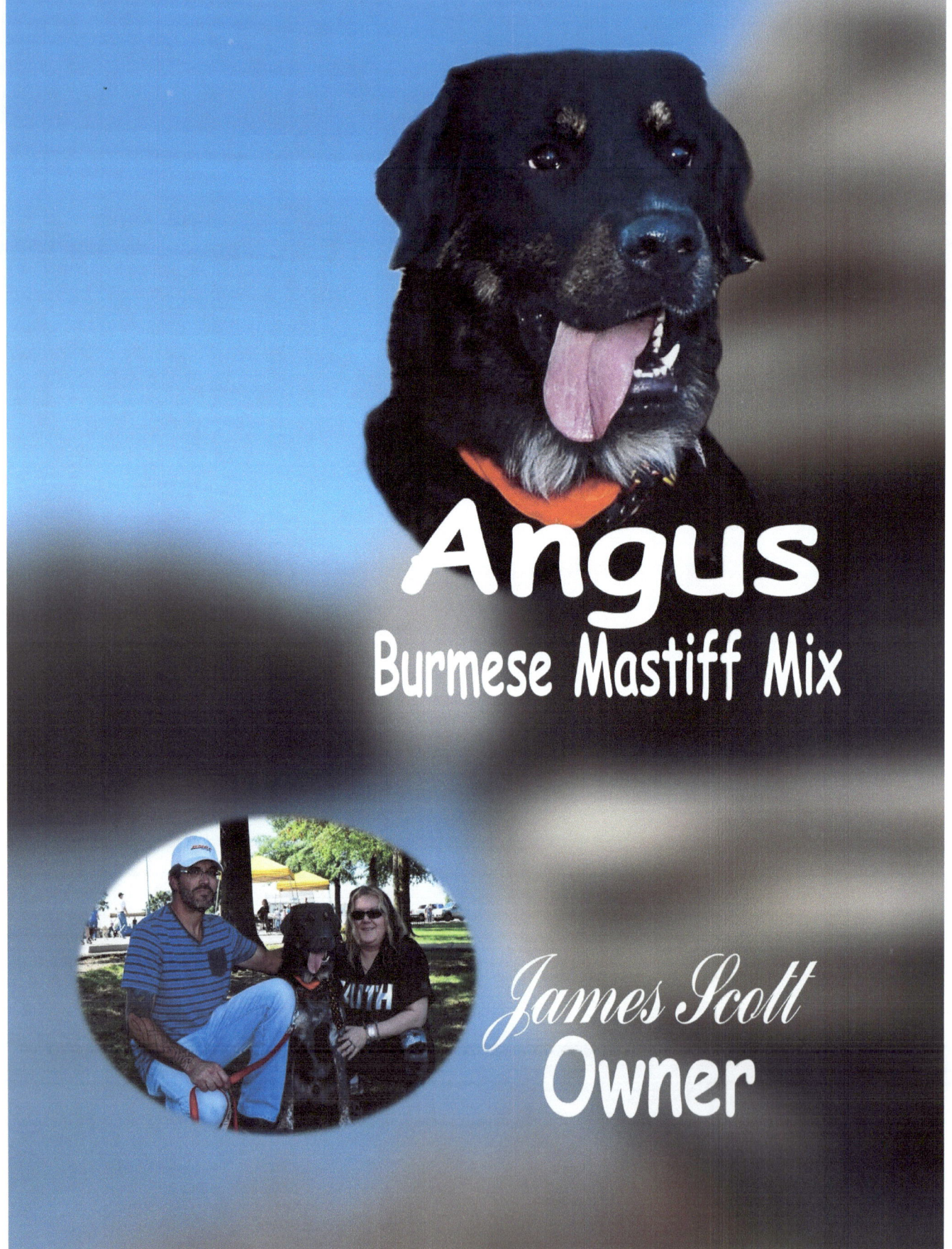

Angus
Burmese Mastiff Mix

James Scott
Owner

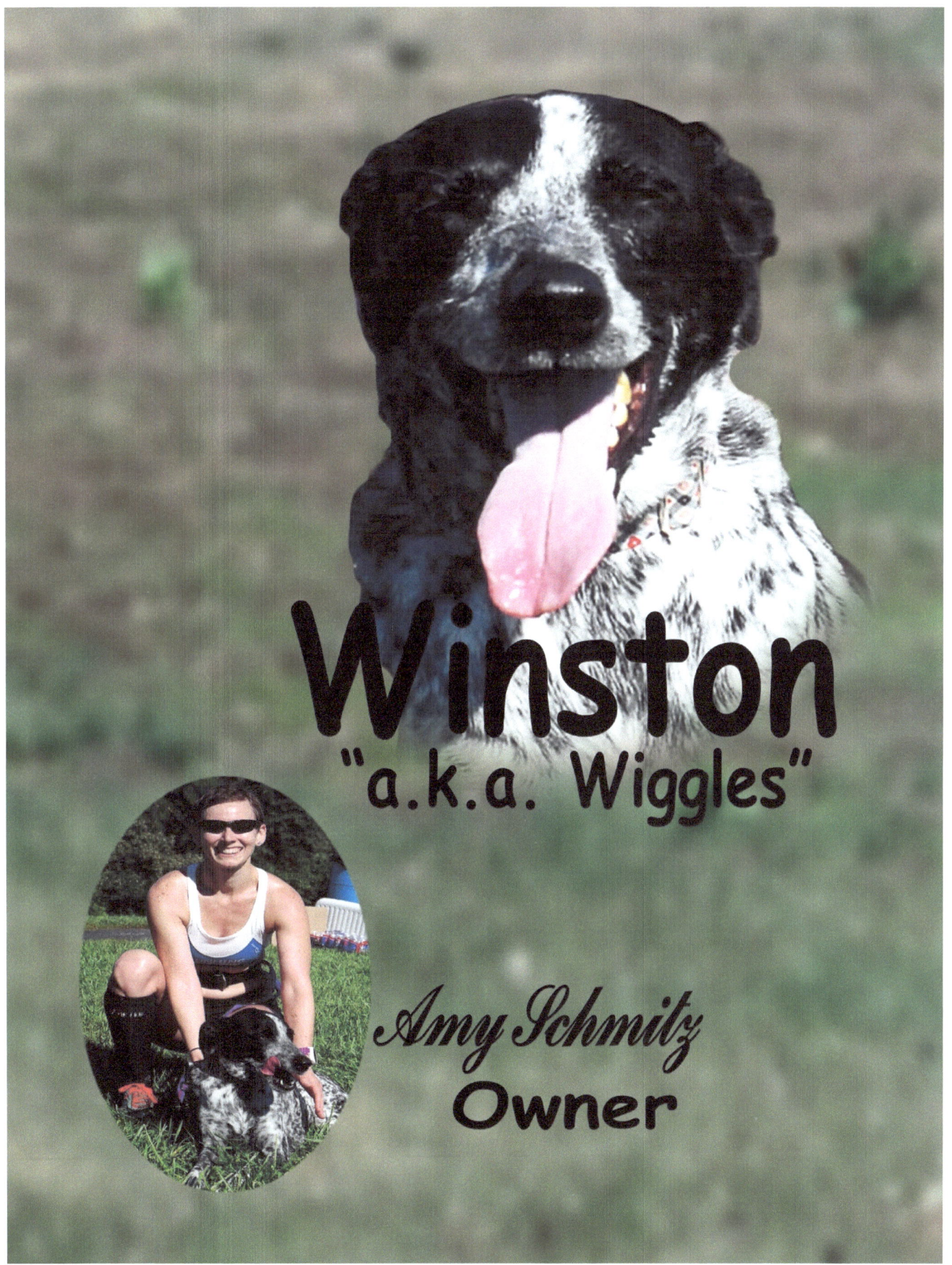

Winston
"a.k.a. Wiggles"

Amy Schmitz
Owner

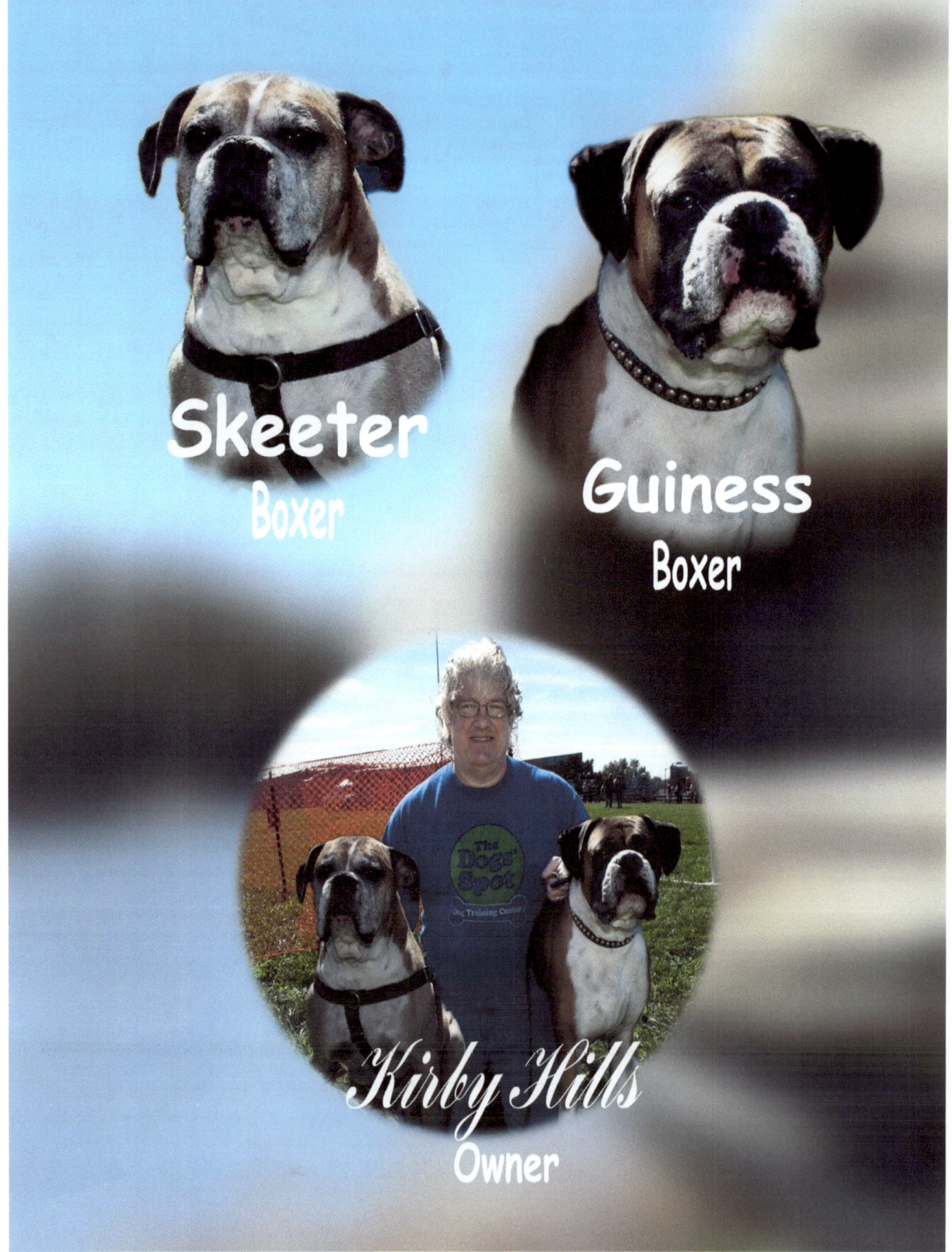

Skeeter
Boxer

Guiness
Boxer

Kirby Hills
Owner

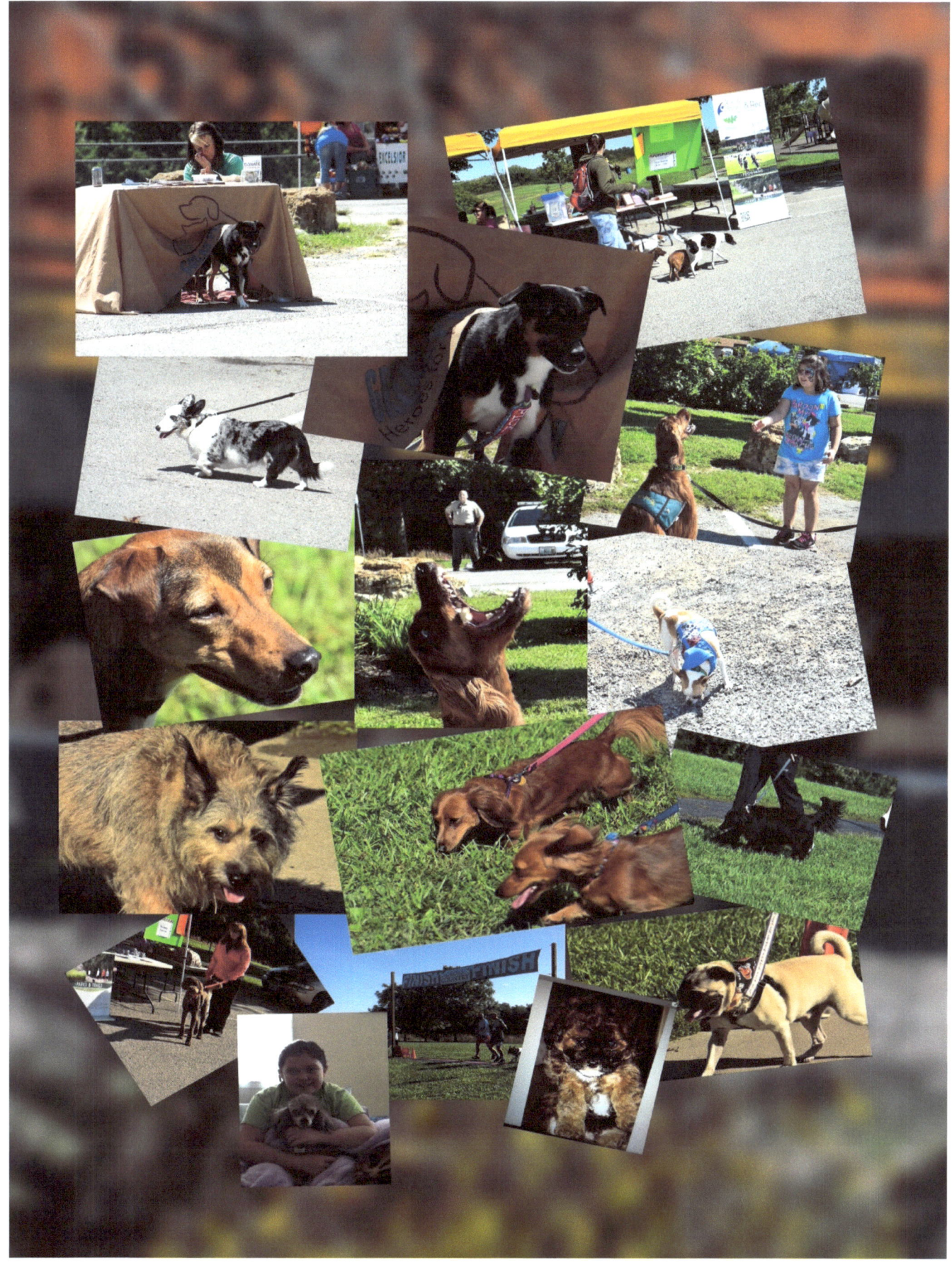